RAILS TO ROSSLARE
THE GWR MAIL ROUTE TO IRELAND

MIKE HITCHES

AMBERLEY

First published 2010

Amberley Publishing Plc
Cirencester Road, Chalford,
Stroud, Gloucestershire, GL6 8PE

www.amberley-books.com

British Library Cataloguing in Publication Data.
A catalogue record for this book is available from the British Library.

ISBN 978 1 84868 701 1

Typesetting and Origination by FONTHILLDESIGN.
Printed in Great Britain.

CONTENTS

INTRODUCTION

Prompted by the efforts of the London and North Western Railway's attempts to win the mail contract to Ireland, the Great Western Railway continually explored ways of competing for this contract in its own right and sharing in the lucrative passenger business that emanated from such mail traffic. Despite many different attempts to compete with the LNWR, who had the distinct advantage of a well-established sea packet port at Holyhead, the GWR did not achieve any real success until the early years of the twentieth century.

Aware that Robert Stephenson had proposed a route along the North Wales coast to Holyhead, Isambard Kingdom Brunel put forward a plan to build a broad gauge line westward from Oxford, via Worcester, Ludlow, and, Montgomery, thence tunnelling under the edge of the Cader Idris to pass Dolgellau and around the shores of Cardigan Bay to a new packet port at Porth Dinllaen, on the Lleyn Peninsula, near Carnarfon, following proposals made by Charles Vignoles in the 1830s. In the event, the Holyhead route was chosen and Brunel's plan came to nothing. The Aberystwyth and Welsh Coast Railway, later to become part of the Cambrian Railways, did try to open a route to Porth Dinllaen but only managed to reach Pwllheli. Cambrian Railways were absorbed into the GWR in 1922 and were never a money-spinner for any railway company that owned them.

If the GWR could not take Irish mail business from the LNWR using North Wales, then the only other alternative was to try to win the mail contract by using a port in South Wales where the company's presence was better established. In order to achieve this, the company offered the prospect of mail transit from Paddington to a new port at New Milford, Pembrokeshire, thence by packet boat to the south-eastern tip of Ireland and on by rail to Dublin. As if to show their commitment to the idea of a rail connection to Ireland, the GWR obtained interests in an Irish railway project from Wexford to Dublin in 1844. Brunel's original intention was for a line that would terminate at Fishguard but, after some work had been carried out in 1851, this project was abandoned in favour of the port at New Milford, later known as Neyland. It was from Neyland that boats operated to Waterford from 1856 after a ten-hour journey from Paddington, a somewhat longer rail-journey time than that of the LNWR from Euston to Holyhead. The LNWR operated trains to Holyhead, a port that had been handling Irish sea traffic since the seventeenth century, and was the shortest crossing to Ireland, with the port at Kingstown being only a few miles from the Irish capital, Dublin, the train service from Euston only taking around 5½ hours at this time. That Fishguard was not developed at this time was largely due to economic conditions in Ireland (the Potato Famine) and a port already existed at New Milford, thereby saving the expense of developing a completely new harbour at Fishguard. A section of railway had, however, been completed westward from Clarbeston Road, and a local company had opened a short branch from Clynderwen (Narbeth Road) to Rosebush in 1876 and was known as the Narbeth Road and Maenclochog Railway. In 1881, the line was bought by the Rosebush and Fishguard Railway, which had no line of its own, and was closed the following year. Despite a change of name to the North Pembrokeshire and Fishguard Railway in 1884, the line remained closed until 1895.

In 1895, the company reconditioned the line and built an extension to Letterston, which virtually exhausted all of its resources. The company approached the GWR in an effort to have them take it over. Paddington was not interested in a line that appeared to be a liability, so the NP&FR looked to the LNWR, who were already well established at Carmarthen, having acquired the former Llanelly Railway line from Llandeilo in 1871. Alarmed at the prospect of the LNWR having access to Fishguard, and possibly developing a port for Irish traffic in competition with the GWR at New Milford, Paddington purchased the line and Brunel's old plans were looked at again. In 1899, the line was extended from Letterston to Goodwick and plans were in hand for a new line to Fishguard to replace the rather poor-quality railway of the NP&FR.

Unfortunately for the GWR, the LNWR had secured the Irish mail contract with the opening of the Chester and Holyhead Railway in 1848, although mail contracts came up for renewal frequently, and continued to hold it without problem. Two factors combined to make the prospect of winning the mail contract from the LNWR much more difficult. The first was the persistence of the broad gauge in South Wales, which caused change of gauge problems, and the circuitous route of trains from Paddington to South Wales. Known as 'The Great Way Round', trains had to go to Bristol, then follow the course of the River Severn to Gloucester and then down the other side to Newport before heading towards West Wales. The LNWR line to Holyhead was much more direct, and so much quicker. While GWR trains to New Milford were taking 10 hours, LNWR trains from Euston to Holyhead were taking only 5¾ hours. Indeed, the total journey time from Euston to Kingstown Harbour (7 miles from Dublin) took an hour longer than the GWR rail journey to West Wales in 1876.

The broad gauge of 7 feet ¼ inches was chosen by Brunel for construction of the infant GWR between London and Bristol, this at a time when the majority of British railways were being built to the 'standard gauge' of 4 feet 8½ inches. Unfortunately, the gauge continued to be used for new construction of the South Wales Railway in order to provide a connection from Paddington to New Milford between 1847, when the SWR was incorporated, and opening in 1851, after the Gauge Commissioners had declared in favour of the 'standard gauge' in 1845. While this may not have been too much of a problem as far as the main line was concerned, many of the South Wales colliery lines had been built to the standard gauge, including the Taff Vale Railway, which had been built by Brunel himself and opened between 1840 and 1841. The colliery companies began to demand that mineral wagons be suitable to work over any railway in Great Britain. Also, there were further problems with interchange of traffic from other railways, which meant that passengers, freight, and mail had to be physically transferred from the standard gauge to the broad gauge. Through carriages from other railways could not operate on GWR lines, creating further difficulties for the company. This proved a distinct disadvantage for travellers who wished to go from parts of Britain not served by the GWR to Ireland using New Milford, putting the

LNWR at great advantage in securing passengers for services to Ireland. Pressure was being applied by the South Wales collieries to convert the main line and, by 1866, it became so great that the South Wales Railway was converted fully by 1872, with the whole route from Paddington being converted by May 1892.

Solving the problems of 'The Great Way Round' to West Wales was to be much more difficult. After all, the River Severn was always going to present a major obstacle to engineers who wished to cross the estuary into South Wales at, what is effectively, its widest point. Also, there was a need to avoid Bristol in order to speed up the railway service still further. Brunel had originally proposed a crossing of the Severn at Hock Cliff when the South Wales Railway was planned, but this idea was vetoed by the Admiralty. The GWR did, however, make attempts to shorten journey times by building branches on both banks of the river and providing a ferry service between Passage and Portskewett. It was not until 1866 that the problem was solved by construction of the Severn Tunnel, the longest in Great Britain at 4 miles 624 yards. The tunnel crosses the Severn between Pilning in Avon and Sudbrook in Gwent, where the estuary is 2¼ miles wide and the range of the tide could be as much as 50 feet. The engineer chosen for the work was Sir John Hawkshaw.

Work on the tunnel began in 1873 with the sinking or a shaft at Sudbrook and the driving or a drainage heading toward the river. Four-and-a-half years later, only the shaft and 1,600 yards or heading had been built. In 1877, contracts were let for additional shafts on both sides and headings on the line of the tunnel. In October 1879, when the headings had nearly joined up, ingress or water from an underground river, the Great Spring, inundated the original Sudbrook workings. A contract was then let to Walker's for completion of the whole works, but it was not until January 1881 that the spring was walled off and the works de-watered.

In April 1881, water broke into the Gloucestershire workings from a hole in the riverbed. This hole was sealed with clay in bags and with concrete. In October 1883, the Great Spring broke in again, and a week later, a spring tide flooded the long, deep cuttings on both sides. A heading from Sudbrook shaft was driven to tap the Great Spring. With water so diverted, the 300 yards of tunnel in which the spring had been walled was completed.

Two 50-inch Bull engines, built by Harvey of Hayle, and installed for dealing with the flooding, still survive – one in the Science Museum, London, and the other stored at the National Museum of Wales, Cardiff. The brick lining was completed for the full length of the tunnel in April 1885, and in September, a special train took a party, which included Sir Daniel Gooch (now chairman or the GWR) through the tunnel.

In 1886, a shaft was sunk beside the tunnel and six pumps with 70-inch beam engines, also by Harvey of Hayle, were installed to deal with the 20 million gallons of water per day, mainly from the Great Spring, at the Sudbrook pumping station. Three of these engines remained in use until the station was electrified in 1961.

The tunnel was opened to traffic on 1 December 1886, the first train being, appropriately, a coal train from the South Wales coalfields, transport of which provided so much revenue for the GWR, from Aberdare to Salisbury. The new tunnel cut the distance from Cardiff to Bristol from 94 miles, via the Midland main line between Bristol and Gloucester, to just over 38 miles.

The problem of avoiding Bristol was solved when the South Wales Direct Line was opened on 1 May 1903, with the new line departing from the main London-Bristol line at Wootton Bassett to junctions with the Bristol-Severn Tunnel line at Filton and Patchway. This new line shortened the distance between London and South Wales by 10 miles and relieved the railway east of Bristol from the overloading that followed the opening of the Severn Tunnel. Much of this traffic was trains of Welsh steam coal destined for the Royal Navy at Portsmouth, and for ocean liners at Southampton.

These new works also did much to improve the timings of Irish boat trains to New Milford. Engineering of the new South Wales Direct Line entailed crossing the southern end of the Cotswolds through the building of a 2 mile 924 yard tunnel at Sodbury, and the construction of three brick viaducts at Winterbourne. The largest of these has eleven spans and is 265 yards long and 90 feet high. This new line has always been known as the 'Badminton Line', following the right of the Duke of Beaufort to stop any train at Badminton; the price the GWR had to pay for putting the new line through his estate.

Following all of these improvements, the GWR was in a good position to offer a much faster service to Ireland and, perhaps, present a serious challenge to the LNWR for passengers and, more importantly, for mail business. All that was now required were improvements to packet port facilities and this was dealt with when a new port at Fishguard was opened.

In the period before the First World War, investment in the new port paid off in a major way, which promised much for the future. However, it had all turned sour by the turbulent 1920s, bringing into question the cost, in time and money, of trying to compete with the LNWR.

In spite of these setbacks, Irish services through South Wales continue to the present day, although without the same frequency as those to Holyhead, which says much about the resilience of the line and, perhaps, those people whose responsibility it was to establish and run these services. Unlike the LNWR, the GWR did not give its trains to Fishguard any specific name and, in later years, most were extensions to expresses like the 'Capitals United' and 'Pembrokeshire Coast Express'.

As well as running trains to Fishguard, the GWR also operated its own steam packet boats to Ireland, which later transferred to British Railways, became part of 'Sealink', thence moved into private ownership.

In writing this book, I have tried to relate the story of GWR's attempts to capture Irish railway business from their great rivals, the LNWR; from ideas which never came to fruition to the great triumph when Fishguard Harbour was opened, the all too brief 'golden years', and subsequent decline, which led to the situation that exists today. I hope that the story of the GWR's attempts to capture this valuable traffic gives as much pleasure to the reader as it has given the writer.

ONE

A NEW PORT AT FISHGUARD

While the LNWR had secured the mail contract for Dublin, via its 'Irish Mail' trains to Holyhead, there was still plenty of passenger traffic to compete for, and the possibility of obtaining a contract for mails to the far south of Ireland, which could be carried by the GWR.

In the early 1890s, the prospect of a through route from London, via Fishguard, to the south or Ireland, first proposed by Brunel some fifty years earlier, was coming near to reality. In 1894, an Act was passed authorising a new company, the Fishguard & Rosslare Railways & Harbours Company, to take over the piers at Fishguard and Rosslare, along with the railways to Wexford in the south or Ireland. On 30 August 1906, a new main line was opened from Clarbeston Road to Letterston and, on the same day, an extension from Fishguard and Goodwick to Fishguard Harbour came into use.

Fishguard was developed to become *the* major port for Irish traffic at, it was hoped, the expense of Holyhead. Much responsibility for the huge expenditure on the harbour rested with J. C. Inglis, chief engineer of the GWR from 1892 to 1903, when he was appointed general manager. Whether the massive expense was justified has been questioned many times, in view of what happened since, for the most important port for Irish traffic was Holyhead at the time of construction, and has always remained so.

From Goodwick, before construction of the new port, there was little, except a rocky shore and sheer cliffs rising straight out of the sea to a height or 200 feet. To provide ground for the harbour station and quay, huge quantities or rock had to be blasted out of the cliff face to create 27 acres of land. At commencement of the project, men were suspended on ropes to drill shot-holes because no foothold could be obtained on the cliff face. A ledge was eventually made and work became easier. In 1902, an American company, Treglown Bros, was engaged to blast rock on a larger scale. This was done with the aid or pneumatic drills making shot-holes, 6 feet by 4 feet, driven horizontally into the rock face down to depths of 60 feet, with cross headings drilled at right angles for a distance of 50 feet. These were packed with up to 10 tons of explosives, electrically fired, and would dislodge up to 100,000 tons of rock at one blast. The first shot was fired on 23 August 1902 and continued until 2,325,612 tons of rock were brought down. Using travelling cranes, the rock was tipped into wagons or moved to where it was needed. Nothing was wasted and all stone was used. Blocks heavier than 1 cwt were used to create a new breakwater, or for other sea defences, while smaller rocks were used for railway ballast, and fine chippings used in concrete making.

The breakwater was laid down in water 70 feet deep and slowly crept out until it reached the original length of 2,000 feet. The base was 300 feet wide and tapered to 70 feet at the top, it being 20 feet above sea level. Every foot of the length required some 650 tons of stone. All the blasting work and removal of rock created a shelf 1,800 feet long and 180 feet wide on which to build the new railway station. The breakwater enclosed 350 acres of sheltered water, providing a deep-water quay for ocean liners, which the GWR planned to attract to Fishguard as they plied between New York and Liverpool.

The new station was laid out on a lavish scale, as befitted the 'main' packet port for Ireland, with two island platforms of 789 feet in length, which were served by four running lines. The platform furthest from the quay was served by No. 1 and 2 lines and the main buildings were placed on this platform, which included the booking offices, waiting and refreshment rooms for all three classes, a bookstall, and other facilities that passengers would require. An office block was built at the breakwater end, away from passengers. The second island platform was served by No. 3 and 4 lines, neither being intended for passengers, but later being used for this purpose. All platforms were covered by an overall roof, which was extended at the breakwater end and over the quay soon after opening. Apart from the new station, the scheme also included low-level galleries to deal with cattle, a power station, a hotel, and houses for staff employed at the station and harbour complex.

The GWR had planned to have the new port and station open for business on 1 August 1906, but there was little likelihood of this date being achieved. It was not until 21 August that the Board of Trade made its inspection of the railway into Fishguard. Having been approved, the station opened on 30 August, after transfer of rolling stock, staff, their families and belongings from Neyland the night before. Cork boats and all GWR ships operating from New Milford sailed round to Fishguard to take up their new stations. A new service to Rosslare was also inaugurated on the same day. New Milford, which reverted to the original 'Neyland', was retained for secondary use and a sleeping car service to and from Paddington still operated until the end of that port's life.

The F&RR&H was jointly operated by the GWR and Great Southern & Western Railway of Ireland, the GWR operating rail services to the West Wales port along with the packet boats, while the GS&WR ran connecting trains in Ireland. Despite amalgamations in both Great Britain and the Republic of Ireland, the F&RR&H remains an independent company, the functions of the GWR and GS&WR now being undertaken by First Great Western and Córas Iompair Eireann respectively. The Fishguard to Rosslare route was now the shortest crossing to Ireland and, perhaps offered a realistic chance of competing with the LNWR for mail and passenger traffic; the shorter sea crossing would compensate for the longer rail journey from Rosslare to Dublin in comparison to the shorter rail journey time from Kingstown (Dún Laoghaire) Harbour.

Attracting mail traffic for Ireland from South Wales had never been easy. Before the railways, a mail packet port had been established at Pembroke Dock in 1824, boats crossing the Irish Sea to Dunmore, with mails and passengers being brought from London by stagecoach. This service was not to last long and was transferred away to Holyhead when the Chester and Holyhead Railway opened in 1848.

Even when the South Wales Railway was opened as far as Haverfordwest, it had problems securing mail contracts for West Wales, never mind contemplating carrying mails to Ireland. Mail for West Wales was carried by horse and cart, operated by Rees and Bowers, before the arrival of the railway. Once the SWR opened in 1853, the railway company wanted Haverfordwest mail traffic but the Post Office was not interested, the contract being retained by the cartage company. The Post Office finally relented after public protest and the first carriage of mail over the SWR was on 20 May 1854, the Post Office paying 3s 7d (18p) per mile between Carmarthen and Haverfordwest. In the following November, the Post Office wished to revert back to cartage, arguing that there was insufficient mail carried west of Carmarthen. Again, following public protest, mails continued to be carried by rail without further disruption. These mail problems in West Wales made the promise of securing a mail contract none too good in competition with the LNWR for traffic to Ireland, via Fishguard. Revenue for such contracts was good enough to make competing for the mails very attractive and the South Wales Railways looked on the Holyhead traffic with some envy.

When the Irish packet port at New Milford was opened in 1856, the GWR had secured a mail contract between London and Waterford in 1854. To serve this new port, a Down mail train left Paddington at 8.10 p.m., reaching New Milford at 8.36 a.m., a two-hour stop being taken at Gloucester. The Up mail left New Milford at 4.26 p.m., altered to 5 p.m. in the mid-1860s. In both cases, letters had to be posted in the early afternoon if they were to arrive in London on the same day. By the turn of the century, with the new cut-offs in place, the Up mail left New Milford at 6.30 p.m. In March 1884, the Down mail was accelerated, leaving Paddington at 9.15 p.m. At the same time, the train carried third-class passengers for the first time, as did all GWR trains at this time. Despite opening of the Severn Tunnel in 1886, mail trains still ran via Gloucester until the Badminton line was opened in 1903, when virtually all express services to West Wales ran via the new route. From October 1894, the Up mail left New Milford at 6.30 p.m., with the old 5 p.m. departure being diverted via Bristol.

With the opening of Fishguard, New Milford was downgraded, but still had a mail service until closure. The GWR transferred its important Irish services and mail trains to the new harbour, providing a mail service to the far south or Ireland, but never succeeded in capturing the Dublin mails, these always going by the Holyhead route.

Mail trains, which connected with boats from Fishguard to Rosslare, left Paddington at 8.45 a.m. and 8.45 p.m., taking 5½ hours for the 261.4 miles. These trains called at Reading, Newport, and Cardiff. They also made a connection for Swansea at Landore. Restaurant cars were run on both services, with a sleeping car provided on the night train, which arrived at Fishguard at 2.15 a.m., an unearthly hour to be awakened from a sleeping berth in order to board the boat. The same train sets could be used for return journeys; the day train returned from Fishguard at 4 p.m., and the night train at 3.25 a.m., reaching Paddington at 9.35 p.m. and 9.05 a.m. respectively. The two night mail trains were advertised as 'The Irish Mail', using the same title as their older LNWR rivals. Was this an attempt to confuse the travelling public and gain passengers at the expense of their bitter competitors?

Fishguard was a great success in the years prior to the First World War, maintaining a thriving Irish service and attracting ocean-going liners. Industrial relations, however, were not as good as they appeared on the surface. In July 1911, there was a strike by Fishguard quay staff in pursuit of increased wages, subsequently granted. Two years later, they tried again, this time without success. A two-day strike was called by the railway unions in 1911, with much trouble at Llanelli, where there were clashes with the army in which two men were killed and the Cork boat train was stopped. Two boat trains arrived at Fishguard with broken windows, and passengers from Ireland were left stranded, though one train did leave the harbour only to be stopped by militant strikers. After being read the Riot Act, the strikers were pushed back at bayonet point and the train went on its way. The following year, the coal strike affected the whole of South Wales and many trains were cancelled.

From opening until the First World War, Fishguard Harbour became increasingly important as a mail port for Southern Ireland, and for ocean liners, which began to call at Fishguard from 1909 on their way from New York to Liverpool, providing mail and passenger revenue for the GWR. While transatlantic traffic stopped when war was declared, it was hoped that it would return when hostilities ceased, a forlorn hope as it transpired. There was, however, plenty of potential business for Irish traffic, but there were to be political and economic problems in the post-war period, which would lead to the decline of Fishguard as the major port of the south of Ireland.

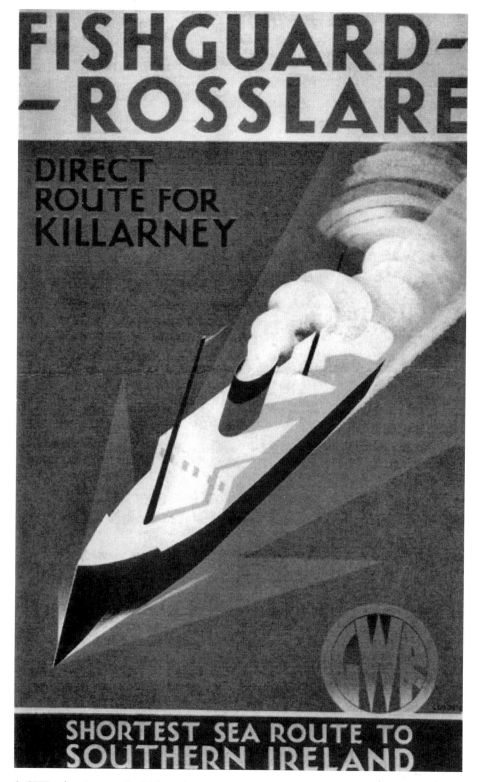

A GWR advertisement for Irish packet services from Fishguard to Rosslare, making the point that the route was the shortest sea crossing to Ireland. (Author's collection)

A general view of the harbour at Fishguard in the early 1950s with ex-GWR 0-6-0 pannier tank No. 6716 shunting. In the background is one of the packet boats, probably the *St Patrick*, built just after nationalisation to replace pre-war vessels. The other is *St David*. The *St David* was built specifically for night services from Fishguard, while the *St Patrick* was intended for winters at Fishguard and summers at Weymouth. When Fishguard Harbour was opened, three turbine steamers, *St George*, *St David*, and *St Patrick*, were introduced on the new service from Fishguard to Rosslare. A fourth boat, *St Andrew*, was added in 1908. *St David*, *St Patrick*, and *St Andrew* were built by John Brown & Co. of Glasgow, and *St George* was built by Cammell Laird of Birkenhead. These boats could achieve speeds of 23 knots and cut crossing times to 3 hours. *St David* lasted until 1933, running in her last year of service as *Rosslare* after her original name had been used for her replacement. The Waterford service, now operated by twin screw steamers *Great Western* and *Great Southern*, built to replace paddle steamers *Milford* and *Limerick*, was transferred to Fishguard as were the boats, the paddle steamers having been built in 1874. Turbine steamer *St George* was sold to the Canadian Pacific Railroad in 1912. At the outbreak of the First World War, the other ships were requisitioned and served as hospital ships, as was *St George* from her new owners. After hostilities ceased in 1918, daylight sailings to Rosslare were discontinued, traffic levels being adequately accommodated on the night service.

A new *St Patrick* was introduced in 1930, to replace the 1906 boat, which had been destroyed by fire, and was used on day services from Weymouth in the summer and night services from Fishguard in the winter. Two further new ships for the Fishguard to Rosslare services, similar in style to *St Patrick* but larger, were built by Cammell Laird and entered service in 1932. These ships took the names *St David* and *St Andrew* from the 1906 vessels that they replaced; *St Andrew* lasted until 1966. A new ship for the Waterford service entered the fleet in 1934. Named *Great Western*, it was the third vessel to carry that name. Built by Cammell Laird, she operated the Waterford service until it ceased in 1959. She then went for considerable conversion into a container vessel and lasted in this form until scrapped in 1967.

During the Second World War, *St Andrew* and *St David* served as hospital ships. *St David* was sunk at Anzio in 1944. *St Patrick* and *Great Western* stayed on the Irish routes, except for brief spells as troop carriers. *St Patrick* was sunk by bombing in 1941 while approaching Fishguard on her normal run from Waterford. This was not the first time that the packet boats had come under attack. Following the creation of the Irish Free State in 1920 and the subsequent civil war, trouble flared at Rosslare in October 1922, causing suspension of sailings, and the packet boat *Great Western* was fired on as it left Waterford Harbour in April 1923. There were no injuries, but services were suspended for two days. (R. Carpenter)

Interior of the railway station at Fishguard with James Inglis, chief engineer of the GWR until 1903 from when he was appointed general manager. It was his idea to build the harbour at Fishguard, and he is seen on the right. (C. McCutcheon collection)

Another view of the interior of Fishguard station in 1909, with passengers waiting to board the train for Paddington. In the foreground is Lord Churchill admiring the facilities at the new station.

Three years after Fishguard Harbour was opened, Cunard liner *Mauretania*, en route from New York to Liverpool, called at Fishguard Bay. Transfer of mail to one of the waiting trains took an hour. The tender *Smeaton*, sent specially from Plymouth, took off 881 bags of mail and parcels. The mail train, with only three mail vans in tow, headed by 'Atbara' Class 4-4-0 No. 3381 *Maine* left at 2.07 p.m. from the specially developed Ocean Quay. Ocean Quay was specially built for transatlantic mail traffic to keep the mail train away from the station itself and allow it to leave Fishguard without going through the station. After making good time to Cardiff, *Maine* was relieved by 'Star' Class 4-6-0 No. 4023 *King George*, which took the train on to Paddington, arriving at 6.40 p.m. This meant that New York mails arrived in London in 5 days, 3 hours and 22 minutes, a record for its day. The passenger train arrived in Paddington 50 minutes later at 7.30 p.m., leaving Fishguard shortly after the mail train. Transatlantic liners continued to call at Fishguard until the outbreak of the First World War. Following the end of the war, shipping lines decided to set down European mainland passengers at Cherbourg and transfer British calls from Liverpool to Southampton and so had no need to call at Fishguard. Thus, the dream of a permanent transatlantic port at Fishguard disappeared and only Irish traffic remained. Perhaps these calls to South Wales made the major shipping companies realise that it was becoming necessary to adopt a port which was closer to London than that at Liverpool, thus making the land journey to the capital so much shorter. In doing so, they contributed to the decline of a famous northern city, now known more for its football team than its once-famous docks. In happier days, Cunarder *Mauritania* is seen with tender alongside in Fishguard Bay. (C. McCutcheon Collection)

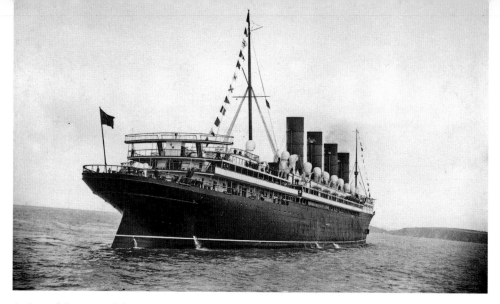

A view of the stern of the *Mauretania* from one of the tenders. In anticipation of a growth in ocean traffic, the GWR made improvements to their main line into Fishguard, which had some severe gradients in West Wales. Beyond Neath was a 1 in 99 climb to Skewen, and a worse climb from Landore to Cockett Tunnel (1½ miles at 1 in 52) followed by a descent of 2½ miles at 1 in 50 to Gowerton. The line also descended at 1 in 50 from Manorowen into Fishguard. It was decided to bypass Neath, Landore and Swansea and connect with a new line to the north with a gradient no steeper than 1 in 120. This was done by securing running powers over the Rhondda and Swansea Bay Railway from Court Sart Junction in order to make use of that company's swing bridge over the River Neath, and then by a new 10½-mile-long line to Morlais Junction South, whence an existing branch would bring trains into Llanelli. The most expensive part of this Swansea District Line was the mile-long Llangefelach Tunnel. It was later planned to cut directly west from Morlais to Pembrey and so cut out the southward diversion to avoid the final 1 in 50 descent into Fishguard, but the First World War intervened and the line was never built. (C. McCutcheon collection)

A long-range view of the *Mauretania* at Fishguard from the hills behind the harbour, showing the harbour wall along with other boats in the bay. The event attracted much local interest, as can be seen here. (C. McCutcheon collection)

Mail tender *Smeaton* is seen loading mail from the *Mauretania* on the inaugural day of the transatlantic service at Fishguard. (C. McCutcheon collection)

Crew and GPO staff of the *Mauretania* and *Smeaton* are seen here transferring the 881 bags of mail from the ocean liner to the tender before sailing back to Fishguard for onward rail transit to London. (C. McCutcheon collection)

Left: Another view of transfer of mails between liner and tender. (C. McCutcheon collection)

Below: The mail tender *Smeaton* sails back to Fishguard Harbour with its bags of mail in 1909. (C. McCutcheon collection)

Special GPO staff were employed on these ocean mail services to sort and take responsibility for the safety of the post, and they can be seen here with a hamper of parcels and letters. (C. McCutcheon collection)

Passengers transferring from the *Mauretania* at Fishguard for onward travel to London were shipped to the railway station by passenger tender *Sir Francis Drake*, seen here as it leaves the liner with its passengers, who will reach the capital much quicker than going on to Liverpool and making the journey from there via the GWR's great rival, the LNWR, to Euston. (C. McCutcheon collection)

Passengers are seen on board the *Sir Francis Drake* as it leaves the side of the *Mauretania*. Note the straw boaters, headwear fashion of the day for men, and the heavy skirts of the ladies. (C. McCutcheon collection)

Sir Francis Drake is seen unloading its passengers at the quay of Fishguard Harbour station, where they will be met by the express train for Paddington. (C. McCutcheon collection)

Baggage tender *Great Western* is seen heading out to the *Mauretania* with the harbour at Fishguard in the background. Another of these baggage tenders at Fishguard was *Pembroke*, built by Laird Bros in 1880 as a paddle steamer for Irish traffic. After an accident in 1896 damaged her engines beyond repair, she was converted to screw propulsion. In 1897, she was temporarily transferred to Weymouth. In 1916, after a spell as a Fishguard tender, she was converted to a cargo vessel and transferred permanently to Weymouth, where she lasted until 1925, by which time she had been in the GWR fleet for forty-two years, longer than any other of the Paddington company's vessels. (C. McCutcheon collection)

The first of the ocean liner special passenger trains to leave Fishguard Harbour in 1909 is seen here, headed by Churchward 'Atbara' Class double-framed 4-4-0's 3402 *Halifax* as the lead engine and 4108 *Gardenia* behind. To the left is another double-headed train with the same class of engines providing motive power. The picture provides a good view of the station as it was when first built. The harbour here was designed so that it could handle up to three packet boats at any one time. (C. McCutcheon collection)

The cavalcade leaves Fishguard station and passes the signal-box. A show of patriotism is observed with the English flag at the window of the box, and this in Wales. How, I wonder, did the local population feel about that? (C. McCutcheon collection)

The train passes the harbour watched by locals. Plenty of boats are present in the area. (C. McCutcheon collection)

One of the coaches used on the new ocean liner trains in 1909. These were typical of the carriages of their day and had the clerestory roofs, which were built by William Dean when he was CME of the GWR. His first corridor coaches had been built in 1892 and were 50 feet long and 8 feet 6 inches wide. By the time Fishguard services started, all trains were made up of such corridor stock. Only twelve years later, when Churchward had become CME, the 70-foot-long Dreadnought coaches were introduced and used on Irish services. All trains had restaurant cars, usually 56 feet long (1896 design) or 68 feet long from 1903. Restaurant cars were well established by the time Fishguard services began, having first been tried in July 1896 on two trains to and from Bristol and Cardiff, and were confined to first-class passengers only. A first attempt to provide refreshments for all three classes was made on the new Cork boat trains, inaugurated in May 1900, which ran from Paddington to New Milford for three days a week. The service was discontinued in October, but restarted in May 1901 when it became a permanent daily train. This train consisted of carriages that were open throughout, with central gangways and a kitchen car from which refreshments were brought to adjustable tables between the seats. Coaches were electrically lit (a new venture at this time) and fitted with new chain communication, replacing an 'endless' cord. Bells to the attendant were also fitted, similar to the push buttons used on modern airlines. Open carriages were not popular with passengers and only a few were built. In January 1903, restaurant cars were supplied for all three classes on Bristol and Cardiff services and extended to other trains very shortly afterwards. By 1902, all South Wales expresses were made up of corridor stock, which were steam heated, a new innovation, which replaced old foot warmers, which were placed under the seats before the train started its journey, and were usually cold three or four hours later. Partition doors between the carriages of corridor stock were kept locked in the early days to prevent passengers of second and third classes invading the privacy of first class, such was the rigidity of the class structure in the late Victorian era. (C. McCutcheon collection)

Interior of the dining car on the ocean liner train, which, as would be expected, is lavishly fitted out and is for first-class passengers. Unlike the passenger coach, this carriage appears to have a high elliptical roof, which would be common on all railway coaches over the next few years. Although transatlantic liners did not return to Fishguard after the First World War, the GWR brought back its restaurant cars on its mail trains and a typical luncheon menu of that post-war period was roast beef with horseradish sauce and potatoes, with cauliflower, followed by fruit and custard, cheese and salad, and biscuits – all for the princely sum of 3s (15p). Sleeping cars for third-class passengers were introduced in the same period that such passengers would be attracted to GWR services to Ireland. These coaches were introduced on mail trains to Neyland. Only first-class sleeping cars had been operating prior to the war. Modern rolling stock was introduced for all Irish services from March 1929. At this time, the GWR had rescheduled its summer services, and the Rosslare boat train left Paddington at 7.55 p.m., a time that was retained for many years. (C. McCutcheon collection)

Sitting in Fishguard Bay is Cunarder *Lusitania* in September 1909. *Lusitania* was the last of the transatlantic liners to call at Fishguard on 14 September 1914, a little over a month after the outbreak of the First World War, never to return. Only a few months later, in May 1915, *Lusitania* was torpedoed by a German U-boat while landing passengers at Queenstown, Ireland, off the Old Head of Kinsale, just as tenders were putting out to meet her. The Germans argued that, although it was a civilian liner, it was carrying war armaments, something that the Government always denied. The incident caused great loss of life; many passengers were American citizens, causing outrage in Washington, going some way to bringing the USA into the conflict in 1917, and bringing about the defeat of Germany when, it could be argued, they were close to victory. Thus, the sinking of *Lusitania* proved to be a grave mistake. Once the war was over, the GWR still retained hopes that transatlantic liners would return to Fishguard and even turned down the possibility that the harbour could become the major importer of oil. The Anglo-Persian Oil Company approached the GWR with a proposal to establish an oil refinery at Fishguard and negotiations took place in January 1915 but soon foundered because the railway company still had dreams of the return of ocean liner traffic. The refinery was eventually established in South Wales at Llandarcy, to the benefit of the Swansea area and at the expense of West Wales. (C. McCutcheon collection)

TWO

ROUTE TO FISHGUARD

The route from Paddington to Fishguard is full of contrasts, as it passes through the suburbs of London and out into the soft country of the 'well-heeled' Home Counties. The line then passes through the county of Oxfordshire as it skirts the warm sandstone structures of the Cotswolds, thence through Gloucestershire, through the famous Severn Tunnel and into the industrial South Wales. As the line passes along, it links the capitals of England and Wales, London and Cardiff, as well as being the route which brought coal from the South Wales valleys to England. Many of the old industries that were the economic lifeblood of the area have long since disappeared, the coal mines closing after the 'Miners' Strike' of the 1980s and giant steelworks at places like Ebbw Vale and Port Talbot have disappeared from the landscape or been rationalised as the once-mighty steel industry has been slimmed down following privatisation. In the glory days, Irish services would have competed with heavy freight trains from the valleys and steelworks as it progressed. Such was the South Wales traffic, it produced vast profits for the GWR, and the fine Welsh steam coal gave the railway company an advantage in performance that other railways could only envy. Sadly, it has all now gone and unemployment in the valleys and South Wales in general has been consistently high, creating many social problems.

Having passed through the industrial areas of South Wales, the line then enters the more rural areas of West Wales, going through towns like Bridgend and Carmarthen. The line here also connects with the coastal resorts of Pembrokeshire and the old port at Whitland and New Milford before running down to Fishguard and connecting with packet boats to the south of Ireland.

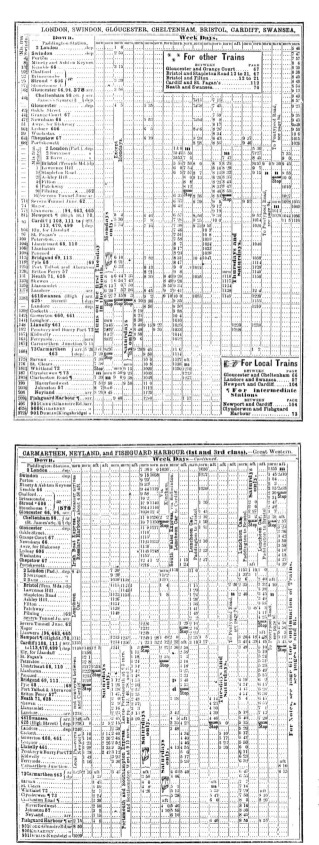

A GWR timetable of 1910 for services between Paddington and Fishguard as well as to Neyland. (Author's collection)

A journey from London to Fishguard and, in earlier days, to Neyland (New Milford) always starts at the headquarters of the GWR at Paddington station. The station has existed since the days of Brunel and is still very much a Great Western structure, despite changes in track gauge, layout, and signalling over the years. The station still retains much of its character, and even though today's passengers travel to Fishguard in modern high-speed trains, it is not difficult to imagine hearing the sharp blast from the chimney of a 'Castle' at the head of a West Wales train in the 1930s. Perhaps leaving Paddington on the way to Ireland could be more exiting than departing from Euston, due to the continuing existence of Brunel's great station, while the grand old structure at Euston has been replaced by a more antiseptic 1960s building; with it went the glamour associated with the great days of the steam railway. Ironically, had Brunel been able to persuade the old London & Birmingham Railway to lay a third rail to accommodate GWR broad gauge trains, Euston may well have been the starting point today and Paddington may not have existed at all. Here, GWR Dean 3206 or 'Barnum' Class 2-4-0 No. 3217 waits to depart Paddington with a westbound train in about 1901. The great train shed is visible in the background. (LOSA)

A Churchward 'Star' Class 4-6-0 departs from Paddington with a westbound train. These locos appeared only a few years after the previous pictured loco, showing how quickly motive power changed in this period. This engine has the 'elbow'-pattern steam pipes fitted in the 1930s. (LOSA)

Successor to the 'Stars' was Collett's 'Castle' Class. Here No. 7000 *Viscount Portal* reverses out of Paddington station after brining in a West Country express. (LOSA)

Collett 4-6-0 'Hall' Class No. 6964 *Barningham Hall* departs Paddington with a relief westbound train in the 1950s. (LOSA)

About to depart Paddington with a parcels train is Hawksworth 'Modified Hall' No. 6964 *Thornbridge Hall* in the 1950s. (LOSA)

Ex-GWR Collett 'Hall' Class 4-6-0 No. 4977 *Watcombe Hall* shunts a parcels van at Old Oak Common shed. The loco shed here was built by Churchward in 1906 to replace a smaller one at Westbourne Park. As it served Paddington, it was a substantial structure with four turntables under one roof and a traverser-type repair shop. The shed became the model for all other new GWR sheds, although none were built with four turntables, most had two, or sometimes only one. (LOSA)

Ex-GWR Collett 'Castle' Class 4-6-0 No. 7005 *Lamphey Castle* awaits its turn of duty at Old Oak Common shed. (LOSA)

Another 'Castle', No. 7026 *Tenby Castle* is at the coaling stage in the 1950s. (LOSA)

Ex-GWR Collett 'Grange' Class 4-6-0 No. 6838 *Goodmoor Grange* sits in the yard at Old Oak Common shed in the 1950s. (LOSA)

Ex-GWR Collett 2-6-0 is seen in the yard at Old Oak Common. As the most important shed on the GWR network, and serving Paddington, Old Oak Common had a large allocation of express engines and other locos, as this allocation for 1950 shows:

Codes: GWR – PDN
BR – 81A

Hawksworth 'County' Class 4-6-0	1000 *County of Middlesex*
	1003 *County of Wilts*
	1008 *County of Cardigan*
	1010 *County of Carnarvon*
	1012 *County of Denbigh*
	1015 *County of Gloucester*
	1021 *County of Montgomery*
	1026 *County of Salop*

1500 Class 0-6-0PT   1500, 1501, 1502, 1503, 1504, 1505.

2800 Class 2-8-0   2826, 2868, 2895.

5700 Class 0-6-0PT   3648, 3685, 3710, 3852, 3853, 4615, 4644, 4666, 4698, 4699, 8707, 8750, 8751, 8753, 8754, 8756, 8757, 8759, 8760, 8761, 8762, 8763, 8764, 8765, 8767, 8768, 8769, 8770, 8771, 8772, 8773, 9700, 9701, 9702, 9703, 9704, 9705, 9706, 9707, 9708, 9709, 9725, 9751, 9758, 9784.

Collett 'Castle' Class 4-6-0	4016 *The Somerset Light Infantry (Prince Alberts)*
	4037 *The South Wales Borderers*
	5004 *Llanstephan Castle*
	5014 *Goodrich Castle*
	5027 *Fairleigh Castle*
	5035 *Coity Castle*

5038 *Morlais Castle*
5039 *Rhuddlan Castle* (oil burning loco at this time)
5040 *Stokesay Castle*
5043 *Earl of Mount Edgcumbe*
5044 *Earl of Dunraven*
5045 *Earl of Dudley*
5055 *Earl of Eldon*
5056 *Earl of Powis*
5065 *Newport Castle*
5066 *Wardour Castle*
5069 *Isambard Kingdom Brunel*
5081 *Lockheed Hudson*
5085 *Evesham Abbey*
5087 *Tintern Abbey*
7001 *Sir James Milne*
7004 *Eastnor Castle*
7013 *Bristol Castle*
7024 *Powis Castle*
7025 *Sudeley Castle*
7030 *Cranbrook Castle*
7032 *Denbigh Castle*
7033 *Hartlebury Castle*

4700 Class 2-8-0   4700, 4701, 4705, 4707.

Collett 'Hall' Class 4-6-0

4900 *Saint Martin*
4923 *Evenley Hall*
4958 *Priory Hall*
4961 *Pyrland Hall*
5918 *Walton Hall*
5931 *Hatherley Hall*
59313 *Haydon Hall*
5936 *Oakley Hall*
5937 *Stanford Hall*
5938 *Stanley Hall*
5939 *Tangley Hall*
5940 *Whitbourne Hall*
5941 *Campion Hall*
5942 *Doldowlod Hall*
5947 *Saint Benet's Hall*
5952 *Cogan Hall*
5962 *Wantage Hall*
5986 *Arbury Hall*
5987 *Brocket Hall*
5996 *Mytton Hall*
6900 *Abney Hall*
6910 *Gossington Hall*
6926 *Holkham Hall*
6932 *Burwarton Hall*
6944 *Fledborough Hall*
6953 *Leighton Hall*

Collett 'King' Class 4-6-0

6001 *King Edward VII*
6002 *King William IV*

6003 *King George IV*
6004 *King George III*
6005 *King George II*
6007 *King William III*
6009 *King Charles II*
6013 *King Henry VIII*
6014 *King Henry VII*
6015 *King Richard III*
6017 *King Edward IV*
6018 *King Henry VI*
6019 *King Henry V*
6021 *King Richard II*
6028 *King George VI*

6100 Class 2-6-2T

6117, 6135, 6137, 6141, 6142, 6144, 6149, 6155, 6158, 6159, 6168.

Hawksworth 'Modified Hall' Class 4-6-0

6959 *Peatling Hall*
6960 *Raveningham Hall*
6962 *Soughton Hall*
6973 *Bricklehampton Hall*
6974 *Bryngwyn Hall*
6983 *Otterington Hall*
6985 *Parwick Hall*
6990 *Witherslack Hall*
7902 *Eaton Mascot Hall*
7903 *Foremark Hall*
7904 *Fountains Hall*
7911 *Lady Margaret Hall*

9400 Class 0-6-0PT

9401, 9402, 9403, 9404, 9405, 9406, 9418, 9419.

TOTAL: 166

After leaving Paddington, the line passes through Royal Oak station, seen here in the 1950s with a DMU in the distance. On the right are the tracks of the London Underground system. (LOSA)

Following Royal Oak is Westbourne Park, seen here in the late nineteenth century with one of the famous Dean Singles at the head of a train for Paddington. A loco shed was established here, which served Paddington until replaced by Old Oak Common in 1906. Westbourne Park shed itself replaced one at Paddington, which was swept away when the present station was built in 1854. (LOSA)

Westbourne Park station in the early twentieth century, with a new Churchward 'Saint' Class 4-6-0 at the head of an Up Bristol express. In November 1862, Westbourne Park shed was the scene of a locomotive boiler explosion, when broad-gauge single *Perseus* blew up. The boiler had not been examined for seven years, a common reason for such boiler explosions in those early days, and was badly corroded. The explosion killed two cleaners and a 'lighter-up', part of the boiler was blown through the shed roof and landed in the carriage siding, which was a hundred yards away. The engine itself was flung a distance of thirty feet. (LOSA)

Following Westbourne Park, the railway passes under a flyover at Ladbroke Grove (scene of a fatal accident a few years ago when a Thameslink train ran through a red light, which was partially obscured, and collided with a First Great Western high-speed train on its way to Paddington from Swansea). At this point, as the line turns west, is the junction for the railway to Birmingham. This line opened as a joint venture between the GWR and Great Central Railway and was constructed to shorten the route between London and Birmingham in an effort to compete with the LNWR, whose line between Birmingham New Street and Euston had been established since the days of the London & Birmingham Railway and was more direct than that of the GWR, whose Birmingham trains had to run via Oxford. When the new line opened, the GWR could offer a two-hour service to Paddington, a similar time to that of the LNWR. The line was moderately successful but was only heavily used when New Street was electrified in the 1960s and London trains were transferred to the GWR route. Once this work had been completed, virtually all London trains from Birmingham went to Euston, with very few going to Paddington. Having passed this junction, the lines enter Acton station, seen here in GWR days with its major goods yards. (LOSA)

From Acton, the lines pass Ealing Broadway. Here it is seen towards the end of the nineteenth century, with a local train for Paddington waiting at the platform. Typical GWR station buildings are visible, the booking office being situated on the road above, a feature of many GWR stations. (LOSA)

A more modern view of Ealing Broadway. The station here was also an interchange point with London Underground services. (LOSA)

The GWR station at West Ealing showing the main station buildings and booking office on the road above. (LOSA)

Just over 7 miles from Paddington, the line passes Hanwell and Elthorne station, seen here with what appears to be a 'Barnum' Class 2-4-0 at the head of a mail train, possibly for New Milford, Fishguard not having opened at this time. (LOSA)

Two miles on from Hanwell is the major junction station at Southall. The Brentford branch joined the main line here and a local train appears to be waiting on the far right. A 'Duke' Class double-framed 4-4-0 is waiting at the main platform as it heads towards Paddington. (LOSA)

On 12 April 1952, Prairie tank No. 6125 is at the head of the 11.30 a.m. Slough-Paddington train at Southall station. Just left is Collett 2-8-0 No. 3851 waiting to go to the loco shed. The shed here had an allocation of some seventy-five locos, mostly local tank engines or freight locos. It is interesting to note how little the station has changed in the intervening years between the two pictures. (M. Whitehouse collection)

The railway at Southall on 25 September 1963 showing the busy loco shed and new motive power, in the shape of DMUs on local traffic. (R. Carpenter)

A mile on from Southall is Hayes and Harlington, seen here at around 1904 with a new Churchward 'Saint' Class 4-6-0 at the head of a short parcels train. It could be that the engine was 'running-in' after being newly built. On the right, the goods shed appears busy. (LOSA)

West Drayton station, the junction with the branch to Colnbrook. On a freight train is a 'Duke' Class 4-4-0. (LOSA)

A little over 14 miles from Padington and the line now enters Buckinghamshire and passes Iver station. The attractive station is seen here in the early twentieth century, the location becoming quite rural. (LOSA)

Ex-GWR Collett 'Castle' Class 4-6-0 No. 5090 *Neath Abbey* passes Iver station with West Wales express. (LOSA)

From Iver, the line then reaches Langley, seen here in the late nineteenth century. Its handsome main building and gardens on the platforms make it a very attractive station indeed. (LOSA)

Exterior of Slough station in the 1930s with motor cars of the day at the station forecourt. Also in view, on the right, are buses, probably operated by the railway company, giving connecting services to towns and villages nearby. Over the next thirty or so years the private motor cars and buses would take traffic away from the railways, causing the loss of many local services and even some longer-distance trains with a general rationalisation of the whole railway system. (LOSA)

Slough station before the First World War. The Windsor and Eton branch joined the main line at this point. (LOSA)

Two miles on from Slough is Burnham, followed a further mile and a half on by Taplow, which was originally named Maidenhead Riverside when the line opened in 1838. This is the point where the railway meets the Thames. To cross the river, Brunel built a viaduct with three long, low arches, which many civil engineers felt would collapse as soon as the first train passed over it. To allay fears of such an occurrence, the railway inspectors insisted that the wooden scaffolding should remain in place when the viaduct opened. The scaffolding was, eventually, blown down by high winds and the bridge remained standing. The Maidenhead Bridge, as it is known, is still in use and carries trains of twice the speed and ten times the weight of those for which it was designed. Perhaps other engineers were jealous of Brunel's design and were attempting to discredit his work. Taplow station is seen here in GWR days. (LOSA)

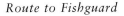

After crossing the Maidenhead Bridge, the line now passes through Maidenhead station, where the line from Marlow and Bourne End met the main line. The line to Bourne End continued on to High Wycombe (as shown on the station name board here), where it met the GWR/GCR line to Birmingham. (LOSA)

Twyford station at the end of the nineteenth century with a local train of three coaches and a brake headed by Wolverhampton-built 0-6-0 saddle tank of 1016 Class constructed between 1867 and 1871. They were later rebuilt with Belpaire boilers and pannier tanks from 1911. Many of these engines were to last for some fifty to sixty years. (LOSA)

In BR days, ex-Collett 'Grange' Class 4-6-0 No. 6861 *Crynant Grange* heads a short train through Twyford station. The Henley-on-Thames branch left the main line at this point. (LOSA)

After leaving Twyford, the line enters the famous Sonning Cutting, seen here on 15 August 1949 with 7006 *Lydford Castle* at the head of an express. The loco still carries the British Railway's lettering in the old GWR style. Construction of Sonning Cutting, like many other railway works at that time, cost many lives among the navvies who were employed in the work, some fatalities occurring during relatively simple operations. One such event happened in the cutting when a young boy slipped in the mud and a horse stepped on his head. (M. Whitehouse collection)

Ex-GWR 'Castle' Class 4-6-0 No. 7025 *Sudeley Castle* is passing through Sonning Cutting on 15 August 1949. After opening, Sonning Cutting was the scene of one of the first major railway accidents. In view of the GWR's excellent safety record, it seems ironic that the company should have been one of the first to have a serious accident and one that would have far-reaching consequences for working-class travellers and railway companies alike. Heavy rain had caused a landslip in the cutting in the early hours of 24 December 1841, which was hit by the regular Down goods train at 4.30 a.m. In those days, goods trains also carried third-class passengers, and the Paddington to Bristol goods train could take some 9½ hours to reach its destination. The train involved was headed by 2-4-0 loco *Hecla* of the 'Leo' Class, followed by two third-class open carriages (one of four wheels and the other of six wheels), one covered parcels van (parcels obviously being more precious than working-class people), and seventeen wagons. The engine hit a mound of earth that had blocked the line, and the two third-class carriages were crushed into the engine by the following goods wagons, killing eight passengers and injuring seventeen others. The railway inspectorate criticised the GWR for having passenger carriages next to the engine and they commented unfavourably on the fact that the carriages were low-sided, exposing passengers to the elements and, in the event of an accident, potentially throwing passengers out of the sides. Even a sudden stop could have this effect. The inspectors also criticised the fact that these carriages had no buffers to absorb shocks in the event of mishaps. These events led to William Gladstone introducing his Railway Act of 1844, which introduced cheap trains for third-class passengers, stipulating that such passengers should be carried on special passenger trains, in covered accommodation, at no more than one penny a mile and at a speed of not less than 12 miles per hour. Although these 'Parliamentary trains' were run at inconvenient times, the railway companies found that such passengers provided an additional source of revenue and conditions were improved for them over time. (M. Whitehouse collection)

From Sonning Cutting, the line enters Reading, a little over 35 miles from Paddington. Reading is the county town of Berkshire and junction of the direct line to the West Country, via Westbury, and to Basingstoke, linking with the Southern Railway, as well as the original main line to Bristol, as the station sign here indicates. A special train for the Reading PSA Society, whatever that is, is seen in Reading station headed by an 'Atbara' 4-4-0. (LOSA)

In 1948, ex-GWR 'King' Class 4-6-0, possibly No. 6019 *King Henry V* is on a Down express from Paddington and is waiting on platform one. (R. Carpenter collection)

GWR 'Hall' Class 4-6-0 No. 4976 *Warfield Hall* waits at Reading General station at the head of an express service. (LOSA)

Ex-GWR Churchward 2-6-0 No. 5391 passes through Reading General station with an empty stock train. The loco was probably acting as station pilot. (LOSA)

A modern view of Reading General station showing colour-light signalling, which replaced GWR lower-quadrant semaphore signals. (LOSA)

After leaving Reading, the line turns north-west as it heads the 18 miles towards Didcot, first passing through Tilehurst, seen here in the late nineteenth century as a train, double-headed by a pair of Dean Singles, runs through. (LOSA)

After Tilehurst comes the very attractive station at Pangbourne, seen here in the late nineteenth century. (LOSA)

Before reaching Didcot, the line still has to pass through Goring, seen here in the early twentieth century. (LOSA)

After leaving the station, the line ran through the water troughs at Goring. Here, on 16 August 1949, ex-GWR 'Castle' Class 4-6-0 takes water at the troughs as it heads an express. (M. Whitehouse collection)

Another 'Castle', No. 7010 passes Goring troughs on 16 August 1949. (M. Whitehouse collection)

A rather grubby Churchward mogul, No. 5326, passes Goring troughs on the same day. The engine still retains its GWR details, although the tender does not appear to show ownership. (M. Whitehouse collection)

Just before arriving at Didcot, the line passes Cholsey station, seen here in the early twentieth century. (LOSA)

Arrival at Didcot, seen here with a train about to depart as a local arrives. Didcot marks the end of four-track working and is the junction of the Oxford line and the original line to Birmingham. A line to Newbury also once ran from Didcot and gave a link to the Westbury route. (LOSA)

An 'Atbara' 4-4-0 waits in the bay at Didcot having brought in a local train, possibly from Newbury. Today, Didcot is renowned as a centre of railway preservation, being the headquarters of the Great Western Society and having a collection of ex-GWR locos, including 'Castles' and 'Halls', along with a selection of tank engines and more mundane locos. The society also has a selection of ex-GWR rolling stock and equipment. (LOSA)

After leaving Didcot, the line turns south-west and then passes through Steventon. The now closed station is seen here with its small main building and pagoda waiting shelter, giving it the feel of a country branch halt. (LOSA)

Heading an Up express through Steventon is GWR 'Castle' Class 4-6-0 No. 5068 *Beverston Castle* on 5 July 1946. Between Steventon and Wantage Road, a train from Treherbert in South Wales was involved in a serious accident on Sunday 20 November 1955, the only serious accident involving a South Wales train on the GWR. The train was on an excursion to Paddington and was loaded with 293 passengers, mostly women from the local Women's Institute, and was made up of nine ex-GWR coaches and an ex-LMS cafeteria car. The train was hauled by 'Britannia' Pacific No. 70026 *Polar Star* of Cardiff Canton shed. On this fateful day, there was a diversion through the goods loop at Milton, 2½ miles west of Didcot, which had a 10 mph speed restriction. The driver did not see the distant signal for the diversion, which was set to caution, although the automatic train control system fitted to all Western Region express engines should have stopped the train before it reached the next home signal. It was subsequently found that the ATC gear did not work as well on a 'Britannia' as on ex-GWR locos. The train ran through the diversion at 52 mph and the engine lurched to the left and crashed down the embankment, taking the track with it. The leading coach fell down the bank, missing the engine, and landed relatively safely in the grass. The second coach crashed on top of the loco and was wrecked by the third coach landing on top of it. The fourth and fifth coaches slewed across the running lines, ripping open as they went and spilling out passengers as the cafeteria car hit and mounted the wreckage. The rear four coaches were virtually unscathed. The disaster killed eleven and injured a further sixty-two, and it took three days to bring everyone out. (E. Johnson)

Wantage Road station, next station after Steventon; like Steventon, this station has long since closed. The area was once famous for its site as the early-nineteenth-century tramway. (LOSA)

Some 10 miles from Didcot is Challow. The station's wooden buildings and goods shed are clearly seen in this 1950s view. (LOSA)

En route to Swindon, the line passed through stations at Uffington, seen here, Shrivenham and Stratton Park. (LOSA)

Shrivenham station is seen here in the 1950s. (LOSA)

Swindon station in GWR days. The station became an important stopping place in the early days of the GWR, and fine refreshment facilities were built to cater for passengers as they waited for engines to be changed on their trains. These refreshment rooms were let to private caterers, whose reputation for quality of food and service declined over the years. As part of the lease agreement, all trains had to stop at Swindon for at least ten minutes. Such were the complaints about the quality of the food and drink served up in these rooms that the GWR was forced to buy out the rest of the lease at great expense to themselves. As well as being on the Paddington-Bristol main line, Swindon is also a junction with a line to Stroud. (LOSA)

An early 1960s view of Swindon station, looking towards Paddington. (R. Carpenter collection)

Another 1960s view of Swindon station, with a local train in the bay, possibly from Stroud. (R. Carpenter collection)

Station frontage at Swindon in 1959. Visible are a Morris Minor and what appears to be a Hillman Californian, a coupé version of the Hillman Minx. Note the poster for 'Rentaset' television hire for 9s 6d per week, a lot of money in those days. Indeed, it could cost around £80 to buy a television in those days, and they were only black and white. (P. Kingston)

The main line through Swindon in 1956, with twin GWR water tanks in the background. Also in view is the church that served the town, which was created by the railway company for its workers. (D. Ibbotson)

The loco shed at Swindon in the mid 1950s, with several of the shed's locomotive allocation in view, including 'Hall' Class 4-6-0s, and there appears to be a 'King' receiving attention just on the left of the picture. As all trains had to stop to change engines at Swindon in the early days, the shed always had a large allocation of broad-gauge locos and was one of the first built by the GWR. It was rebuilt in 1871 as a straight shed with turntable at the rear. The old shed had to be demolished to make way for the expanding locoworks. In the last year of GWR ownership, the shed had an allocation of some 118 locos, from humble 0-4-2 tanks, through 0-6-0 pannier tanks, various freight locos, through to 'Hall', 'Grange' and 'Castle' 4-6-0s. (D. Wilson)

Left: At the back of the loco shed on 19 June 1955 is an unidentified 'Star' Class 4-6-0 fitted, unusually, with a Hawksworth tender. (D. Ibbotson)

Below: Ex-GWR 'King' Class 4-6-0 No. 6015 *King Richard III*, the first of the class to be fitted with a double chimney, is seen outside Swindon loco shed in 1955. (D. Ibbotson)

A front-end view of *King Richard III* outside Swindon shed. (D. Ibbotson)

Ex-GWR double-framed 0-6-0PT waits on the scrap line at Swindon works in 1955. Numbered 1287, it was a member of the 1076 Class, which were originally built as saddle tanks in Wolverhampton in the 1870s. They were long-lived engines indeed. (D. Ibbotson)

An eight-wheeled parcels van is stored at Swindon works in 1957. Swindon, like Crewe and Doncaster, was one of the great railway towns and was chosen as the centre for construction of locomotives and rolling stock for the GWR by Daniel Gooch because it lay approximately halfway between London and Bristol. The works opened in 1843, when 300 workmen moved into a new village built for them, about a mile outside the market town. Two years earlier, the population of Swindon was 2,459, but by 1881 it was 19,904 and the Census of 1851 reckoned that 92 per cent of Swindon's population were employed in the railway workshops. Virtually all of the famous steam locos that ran on the GWR were built at the works in Swindon. Indeed, the very last steam engine built in Great Britain (until the A1 Class Pacific *Tornado* was built at Darlington and completed in 2008) for BR, No. 92220 *Evening Star*, was built at the works, being outshopped in 1960. When the railways were Dieselised in the 1960s, Swindon was involved in locomotive and DMU maintenance until the works closed in March 1986.

An accumulator van, No. W2W, is seen at Swindon works in 1959. Announcement of the closure of Swindon works was made in May 1985, about three months before the works was due to host a major exhibition to celebrate the 150th anniversary of the incorporation of the Great Western Railway, virtually sabotaging the whole event. Employees who were to lose their jobs refused to cooperate with exhibition organisers, and who could blame them? The announcement was particularly insensitive. (D. Ibbotson)

A GWR Dynamometer Car, coupled to a 'County' Class 4-6-0 is seen at Swindon works in 1956. (D. Ibbotson)

Left: End view of the same Dynamometer Car at Swindon works. A 'Castle' Class loco can be seen on the right in this 1956 view. (D. Ibbotson)

Below: An assortment of ex-GWR tenders with the BR 'Lion and Wheel' coat of arms in place, as seen in 1958. (D. Ibbotson)

An ex-GWR 3,000-gallon tender, still lettered 'GW' at Swindon works in 1958. (D. Ibbotson)

Another ex-GWR 3,000-gallon tender with the old company lettering in situ at Swindon works in 1958. (D. Ibbotson)

The accoutrements of locomotive building and repair are seen at Swindon works. Several of the chimneys from ex-GWR locos are placed outside the works, along with several other unidentified items, as they appeared in this 1957 view. (D. Ibbotson)

Five miles from Swindon is Wootton Bassett, where trains to South Wales leave the main Paddington-Bristol line and take the first of the great 'cut-offs' created to avoid Bristol, the Badminton line. Originally built to provide a shorter route for coal traffic from the South Wales coalfields, which was growing apace and was a great source of revenue for the GWR, the Paddington company were also aware that the new route would assist in attracting passenger revenues to its services into South and West Wales. The line is 24 miles long between Wootton Bassett and Westerleigh Junction, passing through two tunnels, the 50-yard Alderton Tunnel and the 2-mile-926-yard Chipping Sodbury Tunnel, pictured here at its west portal. No stations now exist on the line, but there were once several – at Brinkworth, Little Somerford, Hullavington, Badminton, Chipping Sodbury, Coalpit Heath, and Winterbourne. At Westerleigh Junction, the ex-Midland Railway line from Derby, Birmingham, and Gloucester to Bristol Temple Meads joins the GWR line. (D. Ibbotson)

Some 3½ miles on from Westerleigh Junction is Bristol Parkway station, opened in 1972 on the site of the former marshalling yard at Stoke Gifford. As a 'park & ride' station, it was designed to attract motorists on to the trains and off the roads to go to Bristol. Just after leaving Parkway, the line to Temple Meads goes off to the left at Stoke Gifford Junction. Another mile further on, the line to South Wales and Chepstow joins the line from Paddington, Patchway station following straight after. After leaving Patchway station, the line enters the 1,246-yard Patchway Old Tunnel followed by the 62-yard Patchway Short Tunnel just a mile further on. The Up line uses the one-mile Patchway New Tunnel, while the Down line uses the Patchway Old Tunnel. Both old and new tunnels are seen in this 1950 view, which shows the difference in level between the two tunnels. (D. Ibbotson)

Only 2 miles further on is the last station in England, at Pilning, followed by the Severn Tunnel, whose Welsh portal is seen here. The tunnel was the scene of an accident on 7 December 1991 when a 'Sprinter' train travelling from Portsmouth to Cardiff ran into the back of a Paddington-Cardiff train, causing ninety-nine injuries. The accident occurred at the Bristol end of the tunnel and was caused by faulty signalling, even though the whole signalling system here was only replaced a year previously. The 'Sprinter' was travelling at about 30 mph when it collided with the Cardiff train. (D. Ibbotson)

After travelling through the 4½-mile Severn Tunnel, the line emerges into South Wales and approaches Severn Tunnel Junction. The junction was formed from the South Wales main line and the original main line from Gloucester of the 'Great Way Round', often used when the Severn Tunnel is closed for maintenance work. Here, on 19 June 1955, ex-GWR 'Star' Class 4-6-0 No. 4056 *Princess Margaret* is at Severn Tunnel Junction with an SLS special train. (D. Ibbotson)

Just beyond Severn Tunnel Junction station, there was the largest marshalling yard on the GWR, built to deal with huge quantities of coal traffic from the South Wales valleys, later becoming useful for trains from steelworks which were developed in the area. In steam days, the many coal trains were often hauled by 28XX Class 2-8-0s, requiring banking assistance through the Severn Tunnel, which descended at 1 in 90 from Wales and climbed at 1 in 10 to the English end. GWR 'Castle' Class 4-6-0 No. 5082 *Swordfish* (one of the 'Castles' named after Second World War aircraft) is seen passing Severn Tunnel Junction made up of LMS stock from the Midlands to South Wales. (M. Whitehouse collection)

To supply banking engines, a four-road engine shed was established at Severn Tunnel Junction and was opened in 1908. A stud of tank and tender engines were kept here for such duties. A 2-6-2 Prairie tank, No. 4156, is inside the loco shed, alongside what appears to be one of the 2-8-0 freight engines. In the final year of GWR ownership, Severn Tunnel Junction shed had an allocation of 97 locos. (LOSA)

Just beyond the marshalling yards, there was once a small station, known as Undy Halt, followed by Magor, thence to Llanwern where there was a famous steelworks. A little under 9 miles beyond Severn Tunnel Junction, the line crosses the River Usk on a viaduct, which has been rebuilt and widened since the original was built as part of the South Wales Railway. Just beyond is Maindee Junction, where the line to Hereford and Shrewsbury heads north. Some thirty-one chains further on, the line enters Newport station. At Newport station ex-GWR Churchward 2-8-0 No. 2876 heads through with a freight train. (LOSA)

Ex-GWR 2-6-2 Prairie tank No. 5173 waits at Newport station at the head of a two-coach local train. (LOSA)

After leaving Newport, the line heads south-west as it follows the coast on its way to Cardiff, capital of Wales, seen here with GWR 0-6-2. From Newport, through Cardiff, and on to Swansea, the main line passes through what was a massive network of lines that served the South Wales coalfields, connecting them with the GWR and docks at Cardiff, Barry, and Swansea, along with steelworks at Ebbw Vale and Port Talbot. These coalfields were the foundation of the wealth of South Wales, a huge source of revenue for the railway and docks owned by the GWR. Following the 'grouping' of 1923, the local lines that served the collieries were absorbed into the Paddington company. (LOSA)

An unidentified 0-6-0 Pannier tank quietly shunts around Cardiff General station in GWR days. If evidence were needed to show the decline of coal and heavy industry in Great Britain, it can be seen very clearly in this area. Coal, once the staple of the local economy, has declined to virtually nothing since the 1960s, many of the deep mines in the valleys closing after the Miners' Strike of 1984. Along with the loss of the coal industry, the giant steelworks at Ebbw Vale closed in the 1980s, all of which created an economic depression from which South Wales has never recovered. Along with the loss of these industries, many of the old branches disappeared, and only commuter lines that link Treherbert, Coryton, Merthyr Tydfil, and Rhymney with Cardiff remain open. As capital of Wales, Cardiff has three stations: Queen Street, Bute, and Central. Queen Street and Bute serve the South Wales valleys, while Central is on the main line. There was also a loco shed here at Cardiff Canton which, in 1948, had an allocation of 121 locos, including 'Castles' and 'Halls'. Canton was also allocated several BR 'Britannia' Pacifics in the 1950s, which were liked by crews at the shed, an exception among ex-GWR crews, who did not take to them. Today, Canton is a Diesel depot. (LOSA)

After leaving Cardiff, the line turns inland as it heads west, running through Ely, St Fagans, pictured here looking towards Swansea in September 1951, Peterston, Llantrisant (where the Royal Mint is situated) and Llanharan. (R. Carpenter collection)

From Llanharan, the line turns south-west as it heads towards Pencoed, the station seen here in 1963 and looking towards Bridgend. At Bridgend, the line is a little over 20 miles from Cardiff and the station here is an original Brunel structure and is a listed building. At Bridgend, these are lines to Tondu and the Vales of Glamorgan. 7 miles west of Bridgend is Water Street Junction, with connections to Tondu and the railway yards at Margam. The line then turns north-west and follows the coast for 5 miles before reaching the steel town of Port Talbot. From Port Talbot, the line heads towards Neath, passing Court Sart Junction and its lines to the BP chemical works at Baglan Bay and the Swansea District Line. Another 2 miles further and the railway enters Neath. When the South Wales Railway was built, the curves at Neath were not conducive to high-speed running and the stiff gradients locally made heavy demands on motive power. This situation was relieved in 1913 by construction of a bypass line, which crossed the River Neath by means of a swing bridge originally built by the Rhondda & Swansea Bay Railway. Five fixed spans, of plate girder construction, varying in length from 40 feet to 52 feet 6 inches, have been renewed in recent years. The moveable span is a Pratt truss with a curved upper boom, swinging about its centre and resting on a cast-iron roller race, the span being 167 feet 6 inches. Originally operated hydraulically, the bridge is now fixed. It was the only opening bridge of this type in Britain, built both on the skew and on a curve. (LOSA)

After Neath, the line turns south-west, passing Skewen and Llansamlet. At Llansamlet, the line is carried on four 70-foot-span stone arches, which spring from the sides of a cutting. Brunel may have built them to permit a steeper slope to the cutting and save on excavation work. A little over 6 miles from Neath is Landore, site of one of Brunel's huge, timber viaducts. The timber spans were replaced by iron in 1888, and by steel in 1979. Landore is the junction for the line to Swansea, from where the B&I Line's Swansea to Cork ferry operates, a journey of some 10 hours. A Diesel depot now exists at Landore, supplying motive power for services around Swansea. The importance of the station at Landore can be seen here in this view of 4 January 1960. (P. Kingston)

The lines around Swansea were quite complex. Swansea Loop East signal-box is seen on 21 September 1963, facing High Street station; the complex of lines here is also shown. (P. Garland)

Swansea Hafod Junction in September 1953 with a good view of Swansea in the distance. (P. Garland)

Ex-Taff Vale Railway 0-6-2T No. 438 is seen at Swansea Danygraig area, passing Burrows sidings signal-box on 17 August 1935 with a mix of LMS and GWR low-sided wagons. (H. Wheeller)

Just to complete the scene at Swansea, after leaving the main line, is a local train with GWR 0-6-2T No. 6681 providing motive power at Swansea East Dock station on 17 August 1935. (H. Wheeller)

Back on the main line to Fishguard, which bypasses Swansea altogether and heads north-west, entering the 786-yard Cockett Tunnel, some 2 miles west of Landore. Three miles on is Gowerton, followed by Llandeilo Junction a further 4 miles west. Llandeilo Junction is the point where the ex-LMS Central Wales line from Shrewsbury and Craven Arms joins the main West Wales line. Now in West Wales, the line passes Llanelli and Old Castle, where a local line to Cynheidre branches away. From Old Castle, 3 miles away, is Pembrey and Burry Port, whose loco shed, ex-Burry Port and Gwendraeth Valley Railway, is in view with its allocation of 0-6-0PTs in view on 13 June 1954. After leaving Burry Port, the line passes Kidwelly with its junction to Cwmmawr and Ferryside. The line then turns north as it heads towards Carmarthen. (P. Glenn)

Leaving Carmarthen in August 1952 is Churchward 2-6-0 No. 6331 with a train for Pembroke Dock or Neyland. To the left is the loco shed, an allocation of some forty-five locos in 1948. What appears to be a Collett 'Hall' Class 4-6-0 is seen awaiting its next turn of duty. (M. Whitehouse collection)

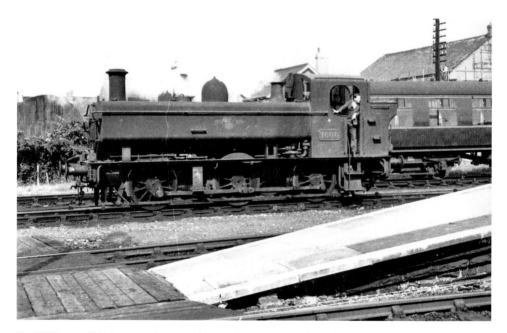

Ex-GWR 0-6-0PT No. 1666 shunts at Carmarthen station in the mid-1950s. At one time, Carmarthen was a junction, having a line to Aberystwyth, which, itself, linked up with the Cambrian Coast Line to Pwllheli on the Lleyn Peninsula in North Wales until Dr Beeching chopped up the system in West Wales by closing the Carmarthen-Aberystwyth line. Before Beeching closed this route, it was possible to travel from South to North Wales without having to enter England. (LOSA)

Ex-GWR Churchward 2-6-0 No. 5353 is at the head of a train waiting at Carmarthen station in the late 1950s. (LOSA)

Ex-GWR Hawksworth 'County' Class 4-6-0 No. 1020 *County of Monmouth* is seen backing out of Carmarthen station with empty coaching stock from Neyland or Swansea in August 1952, possibly an excursion to Tenby. (M. Whitehouse collection)

After leaving Carmarthen station, Carmarthen Bridge Junction is crossed, with the line to Carmarthen station on the left and Myrtle Junction to Swansea on the right. The line to Fishguard bypassed Carmarthen station by means of a short cut-off line that crosses the Carmarthen Bridge, built by Brunel in 1854 with a drawbridge opening span. It was rebuilt in 1910 as a Scherzer rolling lift bascule bridge. (P. Garland)

A view of Carmarthen station and loco shed from the rear of a train bound for Whitland on 31 May 1964. (P. Garland)

12 miles from Carmarthen, the main line enters Whitland Tunnel, with Whitland itself about two miles beyond. Whitland is the junction of a line to Pembroke Dock, which serves the seaside resorts of Saundersfoot and Tenby. Whitland also had its own loco shed, with an allocation of twenty-two locos in 1948. Here, in the early 1960s and awaiting her fate is 0-6-2T No. 6629, shorn of its brass number-plate. Where is that, I wonder? (LOSA)

Leaving the main line, down the branch to Pembroke Dock, is Narbeth station. Seen here in the late 1950s, it still retains its handsome station building and passengers are awaiting a train to Whitland. (R. Carpenter)

At the resort of Saundersfoot is Prairie tank No. 4557 at the head of a Paddington-Pembroke Dock train. 'Manor' Class 4-6-0 No. 7804 *Baydon Manor* is seen light engine on the other platform waiting to return to Whitland. (R. Carpenter)

Departing Tenby for Whitland is the 2 p.m. local headed by ex-GWR Prairie tank No. 5549 in August 1961. (R. Carpenter)

The same loco enters Tenby station with a freight from Pembroke Dock in 1960. Tenby was a popular destination for holidaymakers from the West Midlands at this time. (R. Carpenter)

Between Tenby and Penally in August 1961, a local service for Pembroke Dock is seen headed by 0-6-2T No. 6623. (R. Carpenter)

The little station at Penally looking towards Pembroke Dock in August 1961. As can be seen, the branch was mostly single line after Tenby. (R. Carpenter)

The terminus at Pembroke Dock with Prairie tank No. 8102 waiting to depart for Tenby and Whitland. A member of the station staff can be seen on top of the coach of a newly arrived train. (R. Carpenter)

Pembroke Dock station with the little loco shed in the background, a subshed of Whitland. Light Prairie tank No. 5568 is running back past the signal-box, this scene was recorded on 8 July 1950. (R. Carpenter)

Back on the main line and 5½ miles from Whitland is Clunderwen, where the original line to Fishguard, via Rosebush and Letterston, turned north-west. After the opening of the 1906 deviation line, the old line was retained for goods traffic, going as far as Puncheston. Seven miles along the deviation is Clarbeston Road, which is the junction for Milford Haven, via Haverfordwest and Johnston. In this view, the station at Clarbeston Road is busy with 'Hall' Class 4-6-0 No. 5976 *Ashwicke Hall* passing through the station with a down freight for Fishguard, while a local train with 0-6-0PT No. 9602 in charge waits in the bay, all seen on 4 June 1963. (P. Priestley)

On the branch from Clarbeston Road to Milford Haven, ex-GWR 0-6-0PT No. 9652 waits at Johnston station with a one-coach local for Milford Haven, in 1951. The original line to New Milford (Neyland) turned east from Johnston but the existing line continues south to Milford Haven to serve an oil terminal there. (R. Carpenter)

From Clarbeston Road, the line turns north and is now single track from this point. Nowadays, there are no stations between Clarbeston Road and Fishguard but, in pre-Beeching days, there were stations at Wolf's Castle, Welsh Hook, Mathry Road, and Jordanston. Also, near to Fishguard Harbour, there was a station called Fishguard and Goodwick, seen here in the early 1950s with Collett 0-4-2T No. 1423 on a local auto train. (R. Carpenter)

In connection with the construction of Fishguard Harbour and station, to provide motive power for passenger and freight traffic for Irish train services, and to provide banking assistance on the 1 in 50 climb from the harbour to Manorowen, G. J. Churchward authorised construction of a new loco shed on the Down side of the main line, close to Fishguard and Goodwick station. The new shed was built in red brick and had two through roads, a 65-foot turntable, and coaling facilities. Watering facilities were provided as well at Goodwick platform. First allocations at the new shed included three double-framed 'Bulldog' Class 4-4-0s, Nos 3710, 3714, and 3729. The remainder were saddle tank goods engines, a total of sixteen engines in all. With the arrival of ocean liners, more powerful locos arrived at Goodwick. The first 4-6-0 was a four-cylinder 'Star' Class loco No. 4008 *Royal Star*, which arrived in August 1911, but only remained for a few weeks. Later that year, the first two-cylinder 'Saint' Class 4-6-0s arrived and became the mainstay of express motive power for many years. The first to arrive was No. 2937 *Clevedon Court*, which arrived at the shed on 10 December, closely followed by 2938 *Corsham Court* and 2940 *Dorney Court*, all new from Swindon. A further example of the class arrived a short while later. After the outbreak of the First World War, an assortment of locos arrived at Goodwick shed and the shed had some double-framed 'Atbara' 4-4-0s. Also, a 'Star' was allocated here from November 1914. This engine was No. 4017 *Knight of Liege*, formerly *Knight of the Black Eagle*, whose Germanic name was changed at the outbreak of hostilities. No doubt the new name reflected the fact that Belgium's neutrality had been violated. Another unusual allocation at Goodwick, from August 1916, was one of Churchward's 'County' Class 4-4-0s, *County of Leicester*, the engine staying until 1918. Following the General Strike and Depression, new economies were required and, at Goodwick shed, this meant that the 'Saint' Class 4-6-0s disappeared. The last to go was 2937 *Clevedon Court*, which went on 30 August 1926. Towards the end of the decade, as boat traffic began to improve, Goodwick was allocated new 'Hall' Class 4-6-0s for use on Irish boat services. The first, 4914 *Cranmore Hall*, arrived in February 1929, followed in August by 4942 *Maindy Hall*, both brand new from Swindon works. Two further examples arrived in 1931 and, henceforth, four of the class became the mainstay of the shed. Other 1080s allocated at Goodwick at this time included at least one 43xx Class 2-6-0, along with Class 517 and 'Metro' tanks for local traffic. These last two classes were replaced by 48xx Class 0-4-2 tanks Nos 4823 and 4831, which arrived in the mid-1930s. Towards the end of GWR ownership and just before nationalisation, the allocation at Goodwick shed was as follows:

GWR Code – FGD
BR Code – 87J

Collett 0-4-2T	1419, 1423, 1431, 1452
Dean 0-4-2T	3577
Churchward 2-6-0	5395
Collett 0-6-0PT	5716, 7413, 7747, 9602, 9603, 9760
Collett 'Hall' 4-6-0	5905 *Knowsley Hall*
	5908 *Moreton Hall*
	5928 *Iriaddon Hall*
Collett 'Grange' 4-6-0	6823 *Oakley Grange*

TOTAL: 16

Following nationalisation, Goodwick shed, now coded 87J, had an allocation of four 'Hall' Class locos for boat trains. These were, usually, 5905 *Knowsley Hall*, 5908 *Moreton Hall*, 5928 *Haddon Hall*, and one other. There was also one 'Grange', usually 6823 *Oakley Grange*. Some regular and extra boat trains were handled by locos from Landore shed. Goodwick also had an allocation of a 53xx 2-6-0, a 2251 Class 'Collett Goods' 0-6-0, four 14xx 0-4-2 tanks for auto trains operating in the area, and six 0-6-0 Pannier tanks. In 1957, Goodwick lost its allocation of 0-4-2 tanks as auto train work ceased. As steam declined in the early 1960s, Goodwick was given 'Halls' that had been made redundant from other areas and, in July 1963, the shed even gained two 'Castle' Class 4-6-0s. Steam traction ceased in West Wales from 9 September 1963 and loco sheds at Pembroke Dock and Neyland were closed, Goodwick being retained as a signing on point only. Opposite, in the early 1950s is a view of Goodwick shed with 'Hall' Class 4-6-0 No. 5908 *Moreton Hall* at the coal stage, the turntable is in front, and the entrance can be seen at the bridge, with a Pannier tank waiting outside the shed. (R. Carpenter)

After a four-hour journey from Paddington, the train arrives at Fishguard Harbour, seen here in 1909 with an ocean liner train leaving behind a pair of 'Atbara' double-framed 4-4-0s. Passengers will alight here to join boats for the south of Ireland and on to the railway system that existed over there. (C. McCutcheon collection)

THREE

MOTIVE POWER

The GWR's high degree of standardisation in its locomotives has largely precluded a great variety of motive power on its Irish services to Fishguard, although there were some interesting engines used on trains to New Milford, particularly in the days when the railway was broad gauge.

When the South Wales Railway was opened to New Milford, the line was 7-foot gauge, and Gooch's 2-2-2 'Firefly' Class engines were the mainstay of motive power. These engines were built by Fenton, Murray, and Jackson of Leeds between 1840 and 1842 and were named *Hydra*, *Gorgon*, *Charon*, *Hecate*, and *Medusa*, very much in Greek-legend tradition. All had 7-foot driving wheels and 16-inch x 22-inch cylinders. To help out, Gooch obtained from Robert Stephenson and Co. ten large 4-4-0s of the Lalla Rookh Class with 7-foot coupled drivers and 17-inch x 24-inch cylinders. These engines were not particularly successful, having a tendency to leave the rails. Another engine used in South Wales was a 2-4-0 of the 'Victoria' Class, which had been built at Swindon in 1856 and was named *Victor Emanuel*. All of these engines were scrapped when the broad gauge disappeared in South Wales.

Following conversion to standard gauge, a class of 2-4-0s with 6-foot-6-inch coupled drivers and 16-inch x 24-inch cylinders were introduced, as these suited the South Wales main line very well. These Class 806 locos were the last to be designed by Joseph Armstrong, who was CME of the Northern Division of the GWR at Wolverhampton; the works supplied engines for use in South Wales. These engines were built in 1868 and were based at Neath or New Milford and lasted until the end of the nineteenth century. Other engines operating in South Wales, after gauge conversion, were 2-4-0 'Stella' Class locomotives. These engines were originally built as 2-4-0 condensing tanks for use in the Severn Tunnel and later converted to tender engines, one of which, No. 3201, was sold to the Pembroke and Tenby Railway. It later returned to the GWR after the P&TR had been absorbed and gave the name bestowed on it by its former owners to the whole class. Express trains were, however, usually hauled by William Dean's famous 4-2-2 'singles' and services to New Milford were no exception.

When Fishguard opened, G. J. Churchward was CME at Swindon, and locos whose designs were influenced by him while William Dean was still in charge were already operating Irish boat trains and continued to be used on services to Fishguard. Indeed, two of these 4-4-0 'Atbara' Class 4-4-0s, Nos 3402 *Halifax* and 4108 *Gardenia*, were double-headed to haul the first passenger train from Fishguard to Paddington in connection with the initial transatlantic liner call at the port in August 1909.

In 1904, Churchward introduced his first 4-6-0 locos, the two-cylinder 'Saint' Class, followed by the four-cylinder 'Star' Class in 1907. Both types found their way onto Fishguard services as they became available from Swindon works. They continued to haul these trains until the 1930s when they were replaced by the famous 'Castles'.

The 'Castle' Class 4-6-0s were first introduced by C. B. Collett, who had become CME when Churchward retired in 1922. They were really enlarged 'Stars', but went on to become the most successful engines ever built by the GWR. Originally intended to work expresses to South Devon and Birmingham, some were transferred elsewhere when the larger, more powerful 'King' Class 4-6-0s entered service in 1927. Some 'Castles' began to operate Fishguard trains and continued to be the mainstay of motive power until the very end of steam on the Western Region in 1965. Even streamlined 'Castle' No. 5005 *Manorbier Castle* operated some Irish services as far as Cardiff during the 1930s. All 'Castles' on Irish services terminated at Cardiff with Collett 'Hall' Class 4-6-0s of Cardiff Canton shed taking trains on to Fishguard. BR Standard 'Britannia' Pacifics began to operate between Paddington and Cardiff in the mid-1950s, but were not well received by GWR locomen, except at Canton shed. However, none of these locos ever operated Fishguard trains.

Following the demise of steam, Western Region Diesel-hydraulic locos appeared in South Wales, to be replaced by Diesel-electric locos. These in turn were replaced by 'Inter-City' 125-foot high-speed train sets in 1975, these operating Fishguard trains. Future plans suggest electrification of GWR main lines, and it remains to be seen whether the South Wales main line will be so treated.

Average Train Timings: Paddington-West Wales

DATE	TIME	COMPANY	DESTINATION
1856	10 hours	GWR/SWR	New Milford (via Gloucester)
1884	9 hours	GWR	New Milford (via Gloucester)
1903	7½ hours	GWR	New Milford (via Badminton Line and Severn Tunnel)
1906	5½ hours	GWR	Fishguard
1917	6 hrs 25 mins	GWR	Fishguard
1920	5 hrs 40 mins	GWR	Fishguard
1930	5½ hours	GWR	Fishguard
1939	5 hrs 40 mins	GWR	Fishguard
1947	5 hrs 40 mins	GWR	Fishguard
1955	5½ hours	BR	Fishguard
1965	5 hours	BR	Fishguard
1974	5½ hours	BR	Fishguard
1986	4 hours	BR	Fishguard
1991	5 hours	BR	Fishguard

Waiting to leave Paddington station at the head of an express is one the famous Dean 4-2-2 'Singles'. These engines were built in the 1890s and numbered eighty in total. They had very short lives and were all gone by 1915. (LOSA)

One of the famous 'Atbara' locos at Paddington. It was two of these engines that worked the first of the ocean liner expresses from Fishguard. (LOSA)

One of the 'Bulldog' locos about to depart from Paddington with a westbound train in the early twentieth century. (LOSA)

Interior of Paddington station with 'Star' Class 4-6-0 having just arrived at Platform 8. These locos were introduced by Churchward in 1906 as four-cylinder versions of the two-cylinder 'Saint' Class 4-6-0s. One was allocated to Fishguard for ocean liner traffic in 1909, but soon disappeared. When the first of the American mail trains ran from Fishguard to Paddington, the 'Atbara' used as motive power was changed at Cardiff for a 'Star' for the journey to London. Indeed, four-cylinder GWR locos only operated services to and from Fishguard between Paddington and Cardiff, two-cylinder locomotives completing the journey. (LOSA)

Collett 'Hall' Class 4-6-0 at Paddington. It was usually one of these engines that worked between Cardiff and Fishguard. This view was taken in the 1930s. Many of the GWR express services employed slip carriages as part of the formation and services to Fishguard were no exception and, in 1902, the Paddington to New Milford train, which left London at 9.15 p.m., which also conveyed sleeping cars, slipped carriages at Twyford for Henley-on-Thames. By 1932, the 7.55 p.m. Paddington to Fishguard express slipped carriages at Filton Junction for Bristol and also at Reading. All slip coach services on Fishguard trains had ceased by 1947. (LOSA)

At Cardiff General, Churchward two-cylinder 'Saint' Class 4-6-0 No. 2944 *Highnam Court* is waiting to depart with a Fishguard service. Like the 'Halls', the 'Saints' tended to operate expresses between Cardiff and Fishguard; the loco will have taken over from a 'Castle' at this time. (LOSA)

At the head of a Fishguard-Paddington express is an unidentified 'Castle' Class 4-6-0 passing Southall on 12 April 1952. At the outbreak of the First World War, packet boats were taken over for the war effort, leaving only the Waterford boats to operate across the Irish Sea from 21 September 1914. The following month, the first cancellations appeared on the timetables, with the Waterford service being reduced to three days a week and day sailings to Rosslare being stopped altogether, and it would be a long time before such services were restored. With only old boats in service, timings for the crossing were relaxed. Train services were reduced as a consequence and some boat trains never even reached Fishguard, one such being the 8.45 a.m. from Paddington, which terminated at Carmarthen. Local trains took passengers the rest of the way. The return journey started at Swansea, with local services operating to make the connection. By January 1917, to discourage travel, all sleeping cars and slip carriages were discontinued. Boats were run at the dead of night with just one boat train operating each way. This was the 5 p.m. from Paddington, arriving at Fishguard at 11.25 p.m. The return working was at 6 a.m. with additional stops along the way. (R. Carpenter)

Passing Reading with a South Wales-Paddington express is 'Castle' Class 4-6-0 No. 5004 *Llanstephan Castle* on 4 September 1960. Following the grouping of 1923, the GWR absorbed the South Wales railways, which served the numerous coalfields in the area. Like many areas of industry, the GWR was affected by strikes in the 1920s. Railwaymen supported the miners during the General Strike of 1926. On the first day of the General Strike, thirty passengers from Cork were stranded at Fishguard and forced to return to Ireland. All mail was delivered by road, an ominous warning for the future. The GWR suffered from these disputes, but worse was to come. After the miners' lock-out was over, the country was hit by the Great Depression and output from the South Wales coalfields was drastically cut as demand fell, causing even greater loss of revenue for the railway company. (R. Carpenter)

A Down South Wales express approaches Wootton Bassett on 25 May 1952 with 'Castle' Class 4-6-0 No. 7018 *Drysllwyn Castle* at the head. At the outbreak of the Second World War, two packet boats went off to war and Rosslare services were reduced to three days a week. Trains connecting with these boats were cut to one each way, 7.55 p.m. from Paddington and 6.05 a.m. from Fishguard. Sleeping cars were also withdrawn, never to return. By 1940, the Rosslare boat service was suspended and only an irregular service to Waterford was maintained, as the remaining boats were commandeered as troop carriers. With such an erratic service, wartime mail trains connecting with these boats would often be of considerable length, often containing as many as eleven or thirteen coaches. When peace returned, Waterford services returned to normal on 16 July 1945, with the Cork route reopening on 13 August. It was not, however, until May 1947 that sailings to Rosslare were restarted, operating every other day. On the first day of Rosslare sailings, the Down boat train was said to have run in seven portions. Night boat trains for Rosslare services left Paddington at 6.55 p.m., running on Mondays, Wednesdays, and Fridays only. Mail trains for Neyland had their sleeping cars restored after the war, except for Saturday night Down and Sunday Up trains. The Neyland mail trains, however, only ran between Paddington and Carmarthen, mail and passengers transferring to local services for Neyland. The winter of 1947, with its heavy snowfalls, caused snowdrift problems on the line between Fishguard and Manorowen. Two 'Hall' Class locos coupled together quickly removed the snow with little disruption to traffic. (M. Whitehouse collection)

Ex-GWR 'Castle' Class 4-6-0 heads a Paddington-bound express, the 11.55 a.m. from Pembroke Dock, past Foxhall Junction as it approaches Didcot in the mid-1950s. In the early 1950s, following nationalisation, some improvements were made to Irish boat services operating out of Fishguard. Winter services to Rosslare ran every other night, but became daily in the summer, with additional sailings at the height of the tourist season. Boats to Cork and Waterford ran on alternate days. Down boat trains left Paddington at 3.45 p.m. to connect with Cork and Waterford boats, and at 6.55 p.m. for sailings to Rosslare. Up trains left Fishguard at 3.55 a.m. and 4.55 a.m. Summer reliefs left Fishguard at 3.35 a.m. and 4.25 a.m. All of these trains were worked by Fishguard locomen as far as Cardiff, usually running non-stop. Mail trains for Neyland left Paddington at 9.25 p.m., arriving at 6.50 a.m. (A. W. V. Mace collection)

Ex-GWR 'Castle' Class loco No. 4078 *Pembroke Castle* waits at Cardiff General station at the head of the appropriately named 'Pembroke Coast Express' for Neyland Tenby and Pembroke Dock in 1954. The advent of paid holidays for working people brought a demand for seaside holidays. Along with this, came the Suez Crisis of 1956, which brought petrol rationing and forced car owners to look again at railway travel. Western Region responded by naming as many of its express services as possible to cater for this new tourist phenomenon. In 1953, the Pembroke Coast Express was introduced, mainly to serve West Wales resorts on the line to Pembroke Dock. Another express to be named was the 3.55 p.m. from Paddington to Neyland; this became the Capitals United Express, which lost its name at Cardiff. Some coaches ran through to Fishguard in the peak of the summer months. This train was usually hauled by a BR 'Britannia' Pacific between Paddington and Cardiff. (R. Carpenter)

Passing through Swindon station at the head of a Down Paddington-South Wales express is ex-GWR 'Castle' Class 4-6-0 No. 5091 *Cleeve Abbey* on 4 September 1960. (R. Carpenter)

GWR 'Castle' Class 4-6-0 No. 7016 *Chester Castle* is seen passing Severn Tunnel Junction with a Down South Wales express on 9 October 1948. (M. Whitehouse collection)

Unnamed 'Castle' 4-6-0 is seen at Severn Tunnel Junction with the Up South Wales-Paddington express. In 1970, for a short period, Fishguard became the most important port for Ireland following a fire on the Britannia Bridge, which linked Anglesey with mainland North Wales and cut all rail services to Holyhead from May of that year. Fishguard took all Irish passenger and mail services, and even container traffic was transferred here. The Britannia Bridge was reopened to rail traffic in December 1973 and all Dublin traffic was returned back to Holyhead, Fishguard becoming only a port for car ferry traffic to the south of Ireland. (M. Whitehouse collection)

Ex-GWR 'Grange' Class 4-6-0 departs Carmarthen on 11 August with an express for Swansea. Such two-cylinder locos were the mainstay of express motive power for trains west of Cardiff. (M. Whitehouse collection)

Ex-GWR Prairie tank No. 4122 pilots 'Grange' Class 4-6-0 No. 6804 *Brockington Grange* on the Up Pembroke Coast Express as it leaves Tenby in August 1961. (R. Carpenter)

FOUR

ON TO IRELAND

The GWR was anxious to share in the profits of lucrative Irish traffic and was continually exploring means of achieving this, although the company was not very successful until the early years of the twentieth century. In an effort to secure Irish business, the GWR was not afraid to invest in Irish railways as they were constructed.

An atmospheric railway existed in Ireland, on the line between Kingstown and Dalkey, Brunel visiting the line to see the system for himself in 1844. He was interested in developing an atmospheric railway, whereby trains were operated by use of a piston being drawn through a tube whose air had been pumped out, the train being 'sucked' along. This system eliminated the use of steam locos and was clean and quiet. Brunel planned to use this system on the South Devon Railway where gradients could be steep. The system was not a great success on either side of the Irish Sea.

While in Ireland, Brunel mentioned to the directors of the Dublin and Kingstown Railway, who carried steam packet passengers and mails between these two points, that the GWR planned to build a new line through South Wales and start a new sea passage from Fishguard to Greenore (Rosslare). In order to bring this new service to fruition, there would need to be a railway from Wexford to Dublin and Brunel suggested that the D&K might like to consider a joint venture. The Irish company had already considered an extension of their line to Bray and had completed a survey of the route. The GWR was keen to establish a foothold in Ireland and saw the value of an alliance with such a reputable company. Through Brunel, the GWR pressed for a commitment, announcing plans for a network of lines in the south-east of Ireland, stretching as far as Carlow and Kingstown. To this end, a new company, the Waterford, Wexford, Wicklow & Dublin Railway was formed. In turn, the D&K formed the Kingstown & Bray Railway.

Progress on these projects was hampered by the Great Famine and difficult negotiations between interested parties. Work began on the Bray line in August 1847, with Brunel as consulting engineer; it was not to be one of his most successful civil engineering projects and work was stopped at the beginning of the following year. At the same time, the GWR was not quite as interested in developing a route via Fishguard, preferring to concentrate its efforts on New Milford. The Bray line was eventually completed by William Dargan, who had constructed the original Kingstown and Dublin line, the D&K retaining sole control. The GWR also gave £75,000 towards a scheme known as the Cork City Railway, whose headquarters were at Paddington, and were also involved in the Waterford and Limerick Railway, opened in 1858, as the company was keen to develop lines in the south and south-west of Ireland, which may have drawn traffic away from rival concerns at Liverpool and Holyhead.

Events now centred on Waterford, when the Waterford and Wexford Railway was incorporated in 1864. This scheme envisaged a line from Wexford to Arthurstown, on Waterford Harbour, with a branch to Greenore. A steam ferry was to ply across the river to Passage East where another railway, the Waterford and Passage, sanctioned two years earlier, was to complete the link to Waterford. Only the Wexford to Greenore section was built and this opened on 4 July 1862. At Greenore, the Rosslare Harbour Commissioners built a small pier, which provided some traffic for the railway, but insufficient to make it profitable. In 1889, the line closed, though the owner of a local cement works near Wexford continued to operate a train for his traffic as required.

A plan for a direct Waterford to Cork line failed during the Potato Famine, but a plan for a different scheme was proposed in 1865. Acts were passed for two sections, between Waterford and Dungarvan, and Fermoy and Lissmore but little financial support was forthcoming, so no work took place. The Duke of Devonshire, who had a large estate surrounding his Irish seat at Lissmore Castle, was keen to have a railway in the area. When the Fermoy and Lissmore Railway was incorporated in 1869 he subscribed most of the finance, earning the F&LR the title of the 'Duke's Line'. Apart from the building of a 100-foot-high viaduct over the River Blackwater at Fermoy, there were no major engineering works and the line opened on 27 September 1872. The company never possessed rolling stock and the line was worked by the Great Southern & Western Railway as an extension of its Fermoy branch until 1893, when work was taken over by the Waterford, Dungarven & Lissmore Railway.

The WD&LR Act received Royal Assent in 1872 to complete the final link in a relatively direct route from Waterford to Cork, by way of Lissmore and Mallow. Great difficulty was experienced in raising the capital, and this delayed opening until 12 August 1878. Even then, the company's financial troubles continued. The Duke of Devonshire lent the company £40,000 to ease the situation but, because of incompetent management, he was never paid any interest or repayment. When he demanded his money back, the company was forced to borrow from the Treasury. Twenty years to the day after the first train ran, the line and its neighbour, the Fermoy and Lissmore Railway, were taken over by the Fishguard & Rosslare Railways & Harbours Company to become part of a new through route from Great Britain to the south of Ireland.

In 1894, the F&RR&H took over piers at Fishguard and Rosslare, along with the railway to Wexford. The GWR and GS&WR were asked to support the scheme and, in 1898, an Act gave powers for a railway from Rosslare Strand to Waterford, absorbing the Waterford, Dungarven & Lissmore and the Fermoy & Lissmore Railways. A direct curve, 2 miles in length, from Killinick to Felthouse Junction, to allow through running between Wexford and Waterford was also authorised. Using the Mallow-Fermoy branch of the GS&WR, opened in 1860, through services were planned from Rosslare to Cork. Construction of the 36 miles of new line between Rosslare Strand and Waterford, by Sir Robert McAlpine, began in 1902 and was completed four years later. Charles Brand & Co. of Glasgow built a new pier and viaduct at Rosslare Harbour.

A major engineering feature on the Rosslare-Waterford line was a 2,131-foot-long bridge across the River Barrow, west of Campile, the longest in Ireland. Designed by Sir John Fowler and Sir Benjamin Baker, the bridge was built by Sir William Arrol & Co.

of Glasgow, who were contractors for the Forth Bridge. The bridge had thirteen fixed spans of 140 feet, and an electrically operated swing span, centrally pivoted, giving two openings of 80 feet width for the passage of ships. The cost of the structure was £125,721. Until the 1960s, when mains power was supplied, electricity for the opening span was supplied by a large battery of wet cells charged by a Hornsby paraffin engine driving a dynamo. A second major bridge was also necessary for the direct route from Rosslare to Cork, over the River Suir at Waterford. This bridge was 1,205 feet long with an 80-foot lifting span on the Scherzer rolling system. The contract also went to Sir William Arrol at a cost of £73,250.

On 30 August 1906, the new route opened when the first steam packet service started between Fishguard and Rosslare. The pier area at Rosslare was greatly developed and trains were run to meet sailings on both sides of the Irish Sea. A gas engine was installed at Rosslare in 1906 to generate power for electric cranes on the pier. It was displaced in 1937 when mains electricity became available.

Stations between Rosslare and Waterford were unusual in that they were all built as island platforms, suggesting a GWR influence, which was rare in ireland. The line from Fermoy to Wexford was shown on the GS&WR map as a leased line from the F&RR&H. When CIE decided to close part of the route in the late 1960s, there were legal complications arising from the fact that it was jointly owned by CIE and BR.

Sailing Times: West Wales to Ireland

DATE	TIME	OPERATOR	ROUTE
1856	10 hours	Ford and Jackson	New Milford-Waterford
1874	8 hours	GWR	New Milford-Waterford
1908	3 hours	GWR	Fishguard-Rosslare
1930	3 hours	GWR	Fishguard-Rosslare
1949	3 hours	BR	Fishguard-Rosslare
1974	3½ hours	BR	Fishguard-Rosslare
1979	3 hours 40 mins	Sealink	Fishguard-Rosslare
1990	3 hours 40 mins	Sealink-Stena	Fishguard-Rosslare

At Waterford, home of the famous crystal glass, along with the main line to Dublin, there existed the Waterford and Tramore Railway with J26 0-6-0T at the platform of Tramore station in 1950. (LOSA)

Manor station, Waterford, of the Waterford and Tramore Railway in 1950, with J26 0-6-0T No. 556 on a passenger train. (LOSA)

Over at Cork was the Cork, Blackrock & Passage Railway. Here, 2-4-0T No. 6 waits at Cork Albert Street station with a local train. (LOSA)

A view of Cork Albert Quay station in 1950, showing the main platform and coaches at the arrival platform. (LOSA)

Cork Albert Quay station looking north, showing G1 Class 2-4-0T No. 423 on shunting duties. (LOSA)

Cork Albert Quay with B4 Class 4-6-0T No. 468 in view. Under the Railways Act of 1924, the Cork, Brandon & South Coast Railway, along with the Great Southern & Western Railway, and Midland Great Western Railway were grouped to form the Great Southern Railways in 1925, two years after a similar grouping in Great Britain. This picture was taken in the 1930s, some ten years after the grouping had been completed. (LOSA)

Prior to the grouping, 2-4-0T No. 1 is seen at Cork Albert Quay in 1920. (LOSA)

Ex-Great Southern & Western Railway 4-6-0 is seen on a freight train leaving Limerick Junction in 1950 with a Dublin-Cork train. (LOSA)

GS&WR J15 Class 0-6-0 No. 108 is seen on a passenger train alongside the Tralee branch platform at Mallow station in 1950. When the packet service opened from Fishguard to Rosslare, the GS&WR began running the Rosslare Express to Cork. This train provided a fast limited-stop service until replaced by a stopping train to Limerick in 1966. Special rolling stock was produced for these trains, in the shape of eleven 66-foot-long carriages, running on six-wheeled bogies. All were the same basic design, having wooden bodies mounted on iron or steel underframes. The GW&SR also provided a new refreshment car, with catering subcontracted to Koenig, a German merchant from Dublin. His lease expired in 1916, when the railway company took over the running of the service. This was the most successful cross-country catering service in Ireland and lasted, with little interruption until October 1971. In 1914, the GS&WR opened a branch from Mallow to Fermoy, a 17-mile-long line that avoided Limerick Junction. For many years, this was the route of Rosslare-Cork boat trains until closure in 1967, services then being re-routed through Limerick Junction. (LOSA)

Ex-GS&WR McDonnell D19 Class 4-4-0 No. 15 is seen with the fireman on the tender. The main incentive for the GS&WR sponsorship of the Fishguard-Rosslare project was to capture valuable traffic from England to the south of Ireland. The mail contract came up for renewal regularly and there was fierce competition for it. This was the reason for the opening of the City of Dublin Junction Railway, which created a link between Kingstown Harbour (Dún Laoghaire) and the rest of Ireland. While the GS&WR had kept involvement to a minimum, it benefitted greatly from the direct link between its Dublin terminus at Kingsbridge and Westland Row, terminus of the 'Irish Moil' services from Holyhead. (LOSA)

Terminus of the GS&WR at Kingsbridge, Dublin, in 1928, with coach No. 872 in the right foreground. (LOSA)

On New Years Day 1944, the Irish Government announced plans to acquire the Great Southern Railway and the Dublin United Transport Company, who ran bus services, to form a unified transport system under State control. To bring this into effect, the 1944 Transport Bill was presented to the Dáil proposing that a new company, Córas Iompair Eireann (CIE), Ireland's Transport Company, should take control on 1 July 1944. This first Bill was defeated by one vote and the Dáil was dissolved. The new parliament presented a new Bill, the Transport (No. 2) Bill in 1944, which was passed and the Transport Act became law on 29 November, with the GSR ceasing to exist from 31 December 1944. The new company came into existence on 1 January 1945 and all lines in the Republic became part of CIE. Although the new organisation was having financial assistance from the Irish Government, it was still a private undertaking. In 1949, the Government announced that the entire public transport system in the Republic was to come under State control and a new company, retaining the CIE title, would be formed to manage rail, road, and canal services. This was brought into effect when the 1950 Transport Act became law in June of that year. Here, in the 1950s, shortly after nationalisation, ex-GS&WR 4-4-0, as CIE 330, is seen about to depart from Kingsbridge station with a local train. (LOSA)

Pullman kitchen car No. 192 is seen at Kingsbridge in 1933. (LOSA)

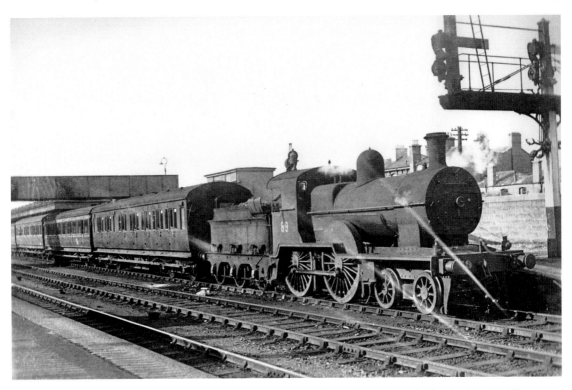

Ex-GS&WR 4-4-0, as CIE No. 69, is seen at Bray in the early 1950s at the head of the Dublin Harcourt Street to Arklow train at Bray station. (LOSA)

Also seen at Bray in the 1950s is CIE Stanier-type non-corridor brake third coach. (LOSA)

Ex-GS&WR G2 Class 2-4-0, CIE No. 657, is seen at Amiens Street, Dublin, in the 1950s. (LOSA)

Another view of ex-GS&WR G2 2-4-0 No. 657 at Dublin Amiens Street at the head of a train in the 1950s. (LOSA)

Dublin Amiens Street with ex-GS&WR J15 0-5-0, CIE No. 132 awaiting its turn of duty. (LOSA)

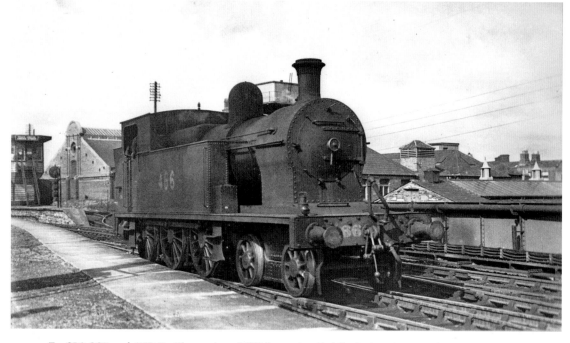

Ex-CB&SCR and GSR B4 Class 4-6-0T (CIE No. 466) at Dublin Amiens Street in the 1950s. (LOSA)

Dieselisation of CIE began in 1955 when locomotives were delivered from Metropolitan-Vickers, Manchester. This was an order for sixty 1200 hp Co-Cos for main line use, and thirty-four 550 hp Bo-Bo's for branch lines. It was the Co-Co engines that found their way on to south of Ireland expresses from Rosslare. Here, a Diesel-headed express passes Dún Laoghaire at the head of an express from the south to Dublin. (Herbert Richards)

Another Diesel-hauled express passes Lansdowne Road, home of the Irish rugby union national fifteen, as it heads towards Dublin. (Herbert Richards)

A push-pull train heads past Dún Laoghaire, near Dublin in 1975. (Herbert Richards)

The RD's sidings, Dublin, in 1971 with a local train passing. In all the time that trains have been running from Rosslare, only one accident has ever been recorded. This occurred on 31 December 1975 when a Rosslare to Dublin train was near Gorey. As the train approached an underbridge, it was dislodged by a road vehicle. The engine jumped the gap created by the accident and came to rest on its side. Three coaches were destroyed and five passengers were killed. (Herbert Richards)

Another local service passes Mennion in 1972. Although the GWR route to Ireland has always been the 'Cinderella' service when compared to that of the LNWR, it has been of great advantage to passengers who have wished to travel to the south of Ireland. Survival of the Fishguard-Rosslare route has often been threatened, not least because of the attraction offered by the Holyhead-Dún Laoghaire route, with its proximity to the capital at Dublin, but the service lives on and seems to be safe for the foreseeable future. (Herbert Richards)

ACKNOWLEDGEMENTS

My grateful thanks go to all who have helped in bringing this project to fruition, including the old Western Region of British Railways at Swindon; Dyfed Record Office, Haverfordwest; the Public Record Office at Kew; the Irish Record Office at Dublin; Coras Iompair Eireann; Birmingham Reference Library; the staff at Penmaenmawr library; and Jim Roberts of Llandudno. Others who have offered their assistance were my late wife Alwen, Bernard Unsworth, and Campbell McCutcheon, who allowed me to have access to his collection of photographs of Fishguard. Further assistance has come from Roger Carpenter and Losa. To everyone, I offer my thanks.

Special thanks go to my wife Hilary, who has had to put up with my taking over the house with paperwork and photographs, and to my son Gary, who I have promised to speak to on many occasions, but have often overlooked while I continued with the project. I hope that he has forgiven me.

To the many others who have been of assistance and that I may have failed to mention, I offer my apologies and thanks.